GOLFER'S G___

THAILAND

MORE THAN 50 COURSES
AND FACILITIES

MICHAEL GEDYE

NEW
HOLLAND

First published in the United Kingdom in 2003 by
New Holland Publishers (UK) Ltd
London • Cape Town • Sydney • Auckland

Garfield House
86-88 Edgware Road
London W2 2EA UK

80 McKenzie Street
Cape Town 8001
South Africa

14 Aquatic Drive
Frenchs Forest, NSW 2086
Australia

218 Lake Road
Northcote, Auckland
New Zealand

1 3 5 7 9 10 8 6 4 2
www.newhollandpublishers.com

ISBN 1 85974 672 1

Edited and designed by Design Revolution, Queens Park Villa, 30 West Drive,
Brighton, BN2 2GE on behalf of New Holland Publishers (UK) Ltd
Project Editor: Nicola Hodgson
Senior Designer: Andrew Easton
Publishing Manager: Jo Hemmings
Series Editor: Kate Michell
Editorial Assistant: Anne Konopelski
Design Concept: Alan Marshall
Cartographers: William Smuts and Patrick Vigors
Production Controller: Joan Woodroffe

Reproduction by Pica Digital Pte Ltd, Singapore
Printed and bound in Singapore by Kyodo Printing Co Pte Ltd

Author's Acknowledgements
I owe a great debt to Lloyd Thomas, Anton Perera, Khun Suchada Yuvaboon, Henrik Lau, Brian Deeson
and Alois Fassbind for their past help and encouragement to learn and understand more about this
fascinating, attractive country and its people. Thanks also to my wife, Tassanee, for her patience and local
knowledge and, in particular, to the Tourism Authority of Thailand and Thai Airways International, for
invaluable assistance in the preparation of this book. I am also grateful to Tony Taylor for his advice and to
Steve Kirk and Parichote Sukriket for the assistance of their annually produced Thailand Golf Guide Map
(662) 995-2300/4.

Photographic Acknowledgements
All photographs taken by Michael Gedye except pages 6, 14, 15, 16, 22, 24, 54, 57, 80, 81, 106, 108, 111, 120, 122, 125, 138, 139,
140, 150, 152, 158 (TAT), page 13 (Thai Airways International), page 33 top (Bangkok GC), page 39 (Lam Luk Ka CC), page 41
(Navatanee GC), page 45 bottom (President CC), page 21 (Thai Muang GC), page 47 (Thai CC), page 53,121 (Rose Garden), page
115 (Mission Hills CC), page 117 (Evergreen Hills GC), page 119 bottom (Nichigo Resort), page 136 (Ronald Fream), page 149
(Southern Hills G&CC).

Front cover: *18th hole, Blue Canyon (Canyon), Phuket*
Spine: *Dynasty Golf & Country Club*
Back cover (anti-clockwise from top left): *The Rose Garden, Bangkok;*
Royal Summer Palace, Bang Pa-In; Laem Chabang, Chonburi; Caddie,
Panya Park, Bangkok; Thai spirit houses.

Title page: *The Rose Garden, Bangkok*

Contents

HOW TO USE THIS BOOK   5

FOREWORD   7

INTRODUCTION: GOLF IN THAILAND   9

THAILAND'S BEST 18 HOLES   18

BANGKOK AND CENTRAL PLAINS   23

Royal Ratchaburi, Dynasty, The Rose Garden, Bangkok Golf Club, Bangsai Country Club, Thana City, Green Valley, Lam Luk Ka, Navatanee, Panya Park, President Country Club, Thai Country Club, Subhapruek, Bangpakong Riverside

EASTERN SEABOARD   55

Natural Park Hill, Natural Park Resort, Khao Kheow, Noble Place, Bangpra, Laem Chabang, Treasure Hill, Pattaya Country Club, Siam Country Club, Phoenix, Rayong Green Valley, Eastern Star, Soi Dao Highland

SARABURI REGION   81

Forest Hills, Mission Hills, Khao Yai Country Club, Friendship Meadows

NORTHERN REGION   93

*Royal Chiangmai, Chiangmai-Lamphun, Chiangmai Green Valley,
Lanna Sports Centre, Santiburi Country Club, Waterford Valley*

WESTERN KANCHANABURI   109

Dragon Hills, Mission Hills, Evergreen Hills, Nichigo Resort

WESTERN REGION   123

*Imperial Lake View, Springfield Royal, The Majestic Creek,
Royal Hua Hin, Palm Hills, Sawang Resort*

SOUTHERN REGION   139

*Thai Muang Beach, Blue Canyon (Canyon), Blue Canyon (Lakes),
Phuket Country Club, Southern Hills, Loch Palm*

OTHER COURSES IN THAILAND   154
ADDITIONAL INFORMATION   155
THAI TOURIST OFFICES   156
INDEX   159

HOW TO USE THIS BOOK

Finding Your Course

The golf courses in this book are presented on a region-by-region basis. To find a specific course, you can look it up in the contents list or the index. Alternatively, if you are looking for a course in a particular location, consult the regional map at the beginning of each chapter then go to the appropriate number within the chapter for a full course description. Within each of the seven regional chapters, the courses are arranged in a loosely geographical sequence, which should assist you in planning an itinerary.

The 53 courses described, plus a further 22 listed, are my personal selection from the 182 golf courses currently in play in Thailand at the time of going to press. There are many plans for expansion in the future, subject to economic conditions. The most highly rated courses are described in depth, including a diagram of the course layout and a full scorecard with hole distances in yards and metres plus total course length.

Golf Courses

Courses in Thailand are measured in yards, and these measurements are given in each entry, together with equivalent distances in metres. If you are accustomed to courses measured in metres, an approximate way to convert yards to metres is to deduct 10 per cent.

The overall lengths shown are the maximum lengths of the courses when played from the back tees. Individual hole distances mentioned in the descriptive text, unless otherwise stated, are also taken from the back tee on the scorecard.

The normal arrangement of tee markers (not always adhered to) is black or dark blue for the back tees, white for the normal tees of the day (men), gold for seniors (men) and red for ladies.

Club Facilities

All the courses included in this guide offer a comprehensive range of facilities for golfers and these are listed in detail in the introduction to each course. The locker rooms, often lavishly furnished, are open to all; it is unusual to find separate changing rooms or other facilities reserved for members. All clubs have lockers for visitors and provide showers and towels, while some additionally offer sauna, Jacuzzi and massage. All clubs have (mostly lady) caddies and you should hire one, whether or not you are taking a golf cart as well. They are not expensive, and are good company and highly professional. All the clubs rent golf sets, also shoes, umbrellas and even folding chairs. On most courses, there are refreshment shelters every three holes or so, which sell drinks and snacks and provide toilet facilities. In addition, all clubhouses will have one or more relatively inexpensive restaurant, some of outstanding quality, usually air-conditioned and often offering a panoramic view over the golf course. Menus normally include an international choice between Thai, Chinese, Japanese and Western cuisine with all-day dining. Expect a selection of beers and spirits but wine may be limited.

Visitors' Restrictions

There are few if any visitors' restrictions, except at those exclusive clubs that require a visitor to be a member's guest. Thai golf clubs, particularly within reach of Bangkok, can be very busy at weekends but most courses have room midweek. Call in advance for a tee time. Few have any handicap requirements or restrictions, which means that play can be slow when a course is busy. More courses are requiring soft spikes but are generally happy to change yours for you on request. There is usually a dress code, so avoid T-shirts and collarless shirts, jeans or beachwear. Thais tend to dress conservatively, preferring long trousers to shorts.

Key to Green Fees

For each course we have provided a rough guide to the green fee applicable, as follows:

B = under 500 baht
BB = 500–999 baht
BBB = 1,000–1,499 baht
BBBB = 1,500–1,999 baht
BBBBB = Over 2,000 baht

These figures are based on the normal full midweek green fee rate charged during the peak golfing season (November to March). Most clubs charge higher rates at weekends; some have 'sport days' midweek with bargain discounts. You may find other discount opportunities, either through your tour operator, ground handler or hotel.

Foreword

Golf! Some people may think that hitting a small ball and then walking after it requires little skill and can hardly prove enjoyable. But those who play this noble game know what an art there is to striking the ball at the right angle to achieve the required distance and possibly make a birdie – or even a hole in one. Golf is a game of skill, yet anyone can play it, young or old. It has therefore become very popular around the world. This popularity has led to the creation of many golf courses in attractive holiday areas, providing opportunities for visitors to enjoy the game in the country of their choice.

Thailand is no exception. In addition to the various attractions and destinations to visit, luxury accommodation to relax in, shopping opportunities galore and delectable cuisine, there are a large number of golf courses of international standard, with superb greens, helpful caddies, first-class facilities and a wide range of services, all set in an exotic tropical environment.

Moreover, these golfing opportunities are not confined to just one region, but are found throughout the country.

As a golfer myself, I know what many of these courses have to offer to both the professional and amateur player. I first met the author on a Thai golf course more than 25 years ago and am sure that, through this publication, you will be able to get a better picture of a truly unique golfing experience.

So, come on and tee off in Thailand soon!

Patpong Abhijatapong
Deputy Governor for Marketing,
Tourism Authority of Thailand

Left: The essence of tropical Thailand – peaceful palms, sparkling sand and clear water. Above: The approach to the par 4 15th at Siam Country Club.

Introduction

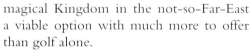

Golf in Thailand

Where in the world can you find guaranteed winter sunshine with midsummer temperatures? Three times as many golf courses as the whole of the Portuguese Algarve and Spanish Costa del Sol put together? Superb modern course design and construction by great names such as Jack Nicklaus, Peter W. Thomson, Arnold Palmer, Ronald Fream, Pete Dye, Greg Norman and many more? Clubhouses like palaces offering exotic menus? Green fees for the price of a round of drinks? Helpful caddies charming you for 18 holes at a reasonable price?

Only in Thailand – the very latest destination on the world holiday golfing circuit and undoubtedly the jewel in the crown. Even travelling there has become easier and cheaper, making this

Left: The par 3 8th hole at Bangpra is downhill across water with a verdant backdrop. Above: Putting on the strategic 16th at Royal Ratchaburi.

magical Kingdom in the not-so-Far-East a viable option with much more to offer than golf alone.

Thailand, formerly known as Siam, has a history dating back over a thousand years. It has been influenced by China and Myanmar but never colonized by the West. Guided by their Buddhist faith, Thailand's gentle, smiling people are noted for their warm hospitality, graceful charm and fascinating cultural heritage. Every visiting golfer should take time 'to smell the flowers along the way' – the gilded temples and vibrant festivals, elegant dancers and unique customs, the rich, aromatic cuisine and delicate handicrafts. They are all part of the enchanting tapestry that makes Thailand the 'Land of Smiles'.

PLAYING GOLF IN THAILAND

Thailand experienced a golfing boom in the early 1990s. This was further fuelled by the rise of part-Thai Tiger Woods. Thailand is now geared to international tourism and offers world-class golf. More than 180 courses, with superb facilities, fantastic value and matchless service, puts the country at the forefront of places to play, with the added value of its amazing culture and history.

When and Where to Play Golf

Golf is playable in Thailand all year round. October through February is the coolest season, especially in the north. Later in the year it can get quite hot, particularly around midday, and from June, rain showers temper the heat, generally in late afternoon. Coastal areas benefit from breezes off the Gulf of Siam and the Andaman Sea.

Below: A mythological yaksa *(demon) guards the gates of Wat Phra Keo and the temple of the Emerald Buddha.*

Courses exist throughout the country, but the greatest concentrations are in the most popular tourist areas – the seven regions covered in this book. From fertile, palm-sprinkled plains to wooded mountain valleys, from sandy beachside to established parkland, there is golf for all at affordable prices. There are few restrictions and a warm welcome wherever you choose. Overseas and local tour operators offer complete arrangements, including transport from your hotel (see p.155).

Travel Tips

Your travel insurance should cover your clubs, if you do take them, but all courses have rental sets as well as umbrellas to shelter you from the sun rather than the rain (there is no need for waterproofs). If you take your clubs, a lockable bag cover is advisable to ensure safe transit and added protection. Golf balls, gloves and other accessories are normally cheaper than in your home country, while bargain 'pickups' are readily available. Take a suitable factor sun cream and lip balm.

TRAVELLING TO AND IN THAILAND
Entry Requirements

Visitors from within the EU, USA, Canada, Australia, New Zealand, and most Middle Eastern and Asian countries, may stay in Thailand for up to 30 days without a visa. They must have a valid passport from their country of nationality. If in doubt, contact your local Thai embassy.

Customs

Visitors may bring up to 200 cigarettes or 250g tobacco in duty free; one litre each of wine or spirits; one still or movie

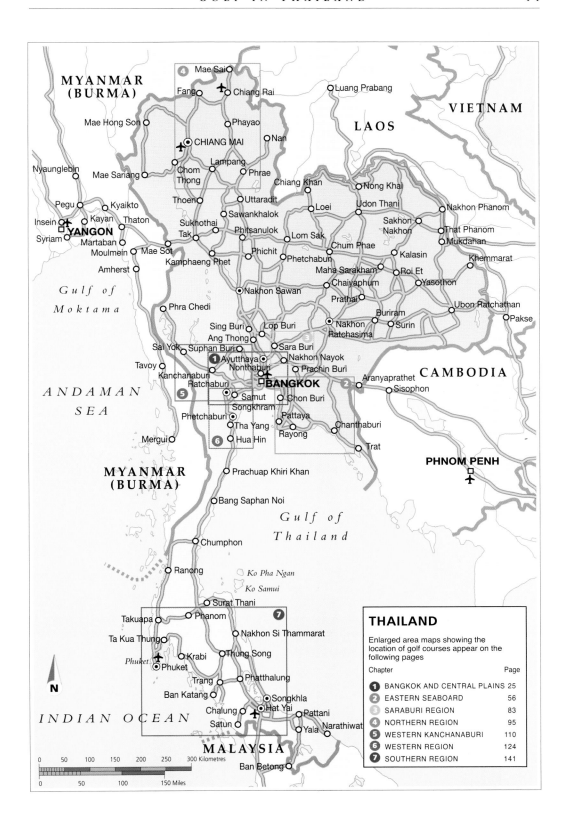

MYANMAR
(BURMA)

VIETNAM

LAOS

Mae Sai
Fang
Chiang Rai
Luang Prabang

Mae Hong Son
Phayao
Nan

CHIANG MAI

Nyaunglebin
Lampang
Chom Thong
Phrae
Chiang Khan
Nong Khai

Mae Sariang
Thoen
Uttaradit
Loei
Udon Thani
Nakhon Phanom

Pegu
Kyaikto
Thaton
Sawankhalok
Sakhon Nakhon
That Phanom

Insein
Kayan
Sukhothai
Phitsanulok
Lom Sak
Chum Phae
Mukdahan

YANGON
Tak
Kalasin
Khemmarat

Syriam
Martaban
Moulmein
Mae Sot
Phichit
Phetchabun
Maha Sarakham
Roi Et
Yasothon

Amherst
Kamphaeng Phet
Chaiyaphum
Prathai

Gulf of
Moktama
Nakhon Sawan
Buriram
Ubon Ratchathan

Phra Chedi
Sing Buri
Lop Buri
Nakhon Ratchasima
Surin
Pakse

Ang Thong
Sara Buri

Sai Yok
Suphan Buri
Nakhon Nayok
CAMBODIA

Tavoy
Ayutthaya
Nonthaburi
Prachin Buri

Kanchanaburi
Ratchaburi
BANGKOK
Aranyaprathet
Sisophon

ANDAMAN
SEA
Samut Songkhram
Chon Buri

Phetchaburi
Tha Yang
Pattaya
Rayong
Chanthaburi

Mergui
Hua Hin
Trat

PHNOM PENH

MYANMAR
(BURMA)

Prachuap Khiri Khan

Bang Saphan Noi

Gulf of
Thailand

Chumphon

Ranong
Ko Pha Ngan
Ko Samui

N

Surat Thani

Takuapa
Phanom

Ta Kua Thung
Nakhon Si Thammarat

Phuket
Krabi
Thung Song

Phuket
Trang
Phatthalung

Ban Katang
Songkhla

INDIAN OCEAN
Chalung
Hat Yai
Pattani

Satun
Yala
Narathiwat

MALAYSIA

0   50   100   150   200   250   300 Kilometres

0   50   100   150 Miles

Ban Betong

THAILAND

Enlarged area maps showing the
location of golf courses appear on the
following pages

Chapter	Page
1 BANGKOK AND CENTRAL PLAINS	25
2 EASTERN SEABOARD	56
3 SARABURI REGION	83
4 NORTHERN REGION	95
5 WESTERN KANCHANABURI	110
6 WESTERN REGION	124
7 SOUTHERN REGION	141

camera with up to five rolls of still film or three rolls of movie film. A reasonable amount of clothing and other items for personal use are also allowed. The import of narcotics or obscene literature is strictly prohibited. No Buddha image may be exported and the export of antiques or art requires a licence. There is no limit to the amount of foreign currency that may be brought into the country. However, foreign currency only up to a value of US$10,000 may be exported, unless declared in writing to the customs officials on arrival. No more than 50,000 baht may be exported without prior authorization.

Health Requirements

No inoculations or vaccinations are required unless coming from or passing through contaminated areas.

Getting There

Bangkok is served by over 50 major airlines, including British Airways, Qantas, EVA Airways and Thai Airways International, all of which fly non-stop from London to Bangkok in approximately 12 hours.

If you choose to fly with the national carrier, Thai Airways International (THAI), all the charms of Thailand welcome you from the moment you reach the airport. One of the world's major airlines, with global coverage, THAI has a deserved reputation for the quality of its service. The author, who has flown on 64 different airlines over the years, has no hesitation in putting THAI top of his preference list.

In-flight service is second to none. Dressed in colourful silk *pasins*, flight attendants offer a level of graceful, hospitable care that is a normal part of the Thai way of life. Personable, multilingual and highly trained, they will make your journey comfortable and memorable. From a gracious *wai* on boarding to a fresh orchid for each female passenger, the Thai experience is with you all the way.

Non-stop flights ensure comfortable early arrival; for example, London to Bangkok is a little over 11 hours. Seat pitch and legroom are among the largest, and in-flight facilities are outstanding. There is a choice of meals in all classes. In fact, the catering is of such high quality that 42 other airlines are served from the THAI kitchens at Bangkok airport.

THAI's Royal Orchid Holidays include complete golf packages within the Kingdom and Royal Orchid Plus offers a travel points programme covering free flights and hotels. In every way, THAI offers outstanding service.

THAI Reservation Office
Tel: (02) 628 2000, 280 0060 (24 hours; Thailand); (020) 7499 9113 (UK)
Fax: (02) 628 2486, 280 0735 (Thailand)

THAI Public Information Centre
Tel: (02) 545 3321 (Office hours only; Thailand)
Fax: (02) 545 3322 (Thailand)
Email: public.info@thaiairways.co.th
Website: www.thaiairways.com

British Airways
Tel: (0345) 222 111 (UK)

Qantas
Tel: (0345) 747 767 (UK)

EVA Airways
Tel: (020) 7380 8300 (UK)

Above: Service with a smile – fine wines go with excellent cuisine on all THAI international flights.

Getting Around

By air

THAI has comprehensive domestic routings, serving 23 airports around the country, from Chiang Rai in the north to Narathiwat in the south. Golfers will be particularly interested in the regular direct flights to Chiang Mai, Chiang Rai, Phuket and Hat Yai. These all take little more than an hour from the central hub of Bangkok.

By road

Car with driver Unless visiting on a package holiday or group tour where transportation is included, getting about is best managed by taxi or chauffeur-driven car rented from your hotel. These are usually available by the hour and are not expensive. Since most golf clubs will be half-an-hour to an hour away from where you are staying, this is easily the most convenient and safest way to travel. The driver will wait for you at the golf club until you have finished your round. Some local companies offer a golf booking and transportation service from your hotel (see p.155).

Self-drive If you have an international driving licence, self-drive is an option. Both local and international car rental companies offer a range of vehicles, although usually only for use in that vicinity. Be warned, however: although the condition of the main highways is generally excellent, smaller roads can be a lot worse and usually have direction signs only in Thai. Sudden storms in the rainy season can be a real problem. Off the main roads and into the countryside, petrol stations are sparse. Thailand drives

Above: The much revered bronze Phra Buddha Chinaraj in Wat Mahathat at Phitsanulok.

on the left-hand side of the road – at least most of the time. Driving standards tend to border on the suicidal, with overtaking on the inside, on bends and crests of hills the norm. Local knowledge and anticipation are vital, since all drivers believe that they have the right of way.

Buses Intercity buses are inexpensive and the VIP variety have reclining seats, luggage space and air conditioning. Other buses in major towns can be hot, crowded and have no space for baggage. However, no buses travel via golf clubs.

By rail

There is an efficient rail system between main towns with seating in three classes on the domestic express trains. Tickets can be purchased in advance.

ACCOMMODATION

Many visitors come to Thailand on a package tour, which includes hotel accommodation in one or more location. The independent traveller will find excellent hotels in all main cities with high levels of service and value. Many golf resorts also have adjacent accommodation. Recommendations are included throughout this book. Alternatively, the local office of the Tourism Authority of Thailand (see pp.156–58) offers lists of accommodation and rates.

FOOD AND DRINK

Thailand has a world-renowned reputation for its excellent cuisine. Based on historical influences from China, Myanmar and Malaysia, and enhanced by a wide range of fresh local ingredients, herbs and spices, the choice is varied and exciting. There are considerable regional variations. 'Sticky' rice is found in the north and the scented jasmine variety is found further south. You can also choose between the varieties of sausage, pork and chicken dishes or the natural attractions of freshly caught fish and seafood. Few can fail to be enticed by the range of subtle (and sometimes quite spicy) flavours. Most hotels and golf clubs also offer a range of Japanese, Chinese and Western dishes, but no visitor should avoid the enticements of delicate Thai soups, curries laced with coconut milk, stir-fried vegetables or exotic fresh fruits that form only part of this unique culinary adventure. (See pages 150 and 152.)

Many Thais do not consume alcohol, preferring sweet soft drinks and bottled water. Alcoholic drinks are, however, freely available. They range from inexpensive, locally produced beers, with Thai and international brand names, to the full range of imported wines and spirits. There are also brands of local Thai whisky. These tend to be cheap and are an acquired taste. In contrast to many countries, the Thai taxation system makes premium Scotch whisky a cheaper drink than quite moderate imported wine.

In many restaurants, particularly in provincial regions, you will find that the menu lists soft drinks, beer and whisky. The latter is sold by the bottle rather than the glass. Outside Bangkok, wine tends to be available only in better-class hotels and tourist restaurants. For drinking water, it is advisable to stick to the bottled variety.

TRAVEL FACTS AND TIPS

Currency

The unit of currency is the baht. Each baht consists of 100 satang, although these small coins rarely figure in any tourist transaction. Other coins are 1, 2, 5 and 10 baht. Bank notes are valued at 20, 50, 100, 500 and 1,000 baht.

Travellers Cheques and Credit Cards

Travellers cheques can be exchanged in banks, money exchange kiosks and in most hotels, although here the rate will be lower. You will need to show your passport for any transaction.

The most widely accepted international credit cards are American Express, Diners, Carte Blanche, Visa and Mastercard. Smaller shops may insist on cash. Automatic cash machines are available nationally 24 hours a day.

Tipping

It is customary to tip porters and hotel personnel for good service. In restaurants, a tip of 10-15 per cent is appreciated, this is the case particularly if no service charge is added. Major hotels include a service

Below: Shimmering and colourful, handmade Thai silk represents craftsmanship at its glorious best.

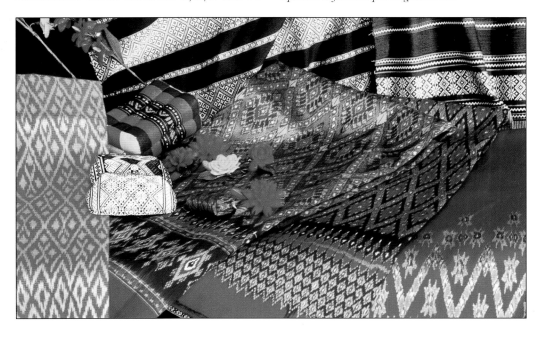

Above: Hand-painted parasols, made in the Chiang Mai craft village of Bo San, are unique.

charge on bills. It is not expected to tip taxi or limousine drivers. At the golf club, the caddies should get a tip of between 50 per cent and 100 per cent of their very reasonable fee, depending on service.

Business Hours
Most government offices open from Monday to Friday between 08.30 and 16.30 with a lunch break from noon to 13.00, except on public holidays. Many stores open 12 hours a day, seven days a week. Banking hours are 09.30 to 15.30, Monday to Friday.

What to Wear
Thailand has a tropical climate with three seasons: hot from March through May, rainy from June to September and cool from October through February. Light, loose cotton clothing is best with possibly a sweater for evenings in the cool season. Certain restaurants require a jacket and tie. Thais generally dress modestly and visitors should avoid wearing brief or revealing attire, particularly when visiting holy places. Golf clubs observe normal dress codes. Shoes should be removed before entering temples and private Thai homes.

Etiquette
Thai people place great store by good manners and the virtues of patience, tolerance, calmness, helpfulness and cleanliness. They also deeply honour and respect their royal family, Buddha images and the elderly, especially members of their own family. An awareness of this will make life much easier for the visitor. There are a number of social gaffes that one should aim to avoid. Thais greet with a *wai* rather than shaking hands (see p.133). In public, it is considered bad form to raise one's voice or have an argument, to dress immodestly, for a man to touch a woman,

or for a couple to kiss or hold hands. The head is thought to be the repository of the soul and should not be touched. Pointing with the foot is considered rude. When passing one another, Thais dip low in order not to 'look down' on the other person, especially if he or she is older or more senior. Monks are forbidden to touch or be touched by a woman or to directly accept anything from one.

Communications

Post offices are open from 08.00 to 16.30 Monday to Friday and from 09.00 to 13.00 on Saturdays. The Central GPO in Bangkok remains open until 18.00 weekdays and from 09.00 to 13.00 on Saturdays, Sundays and public holidays. Telegram and recorded delivery services are available. It is not recommended to send anything valuable by letter; also expect the post to take a bit longer than you may be used to elsewhere.

Leading hotels offer IDD telephone services from your room plus fax and other business services. Public kiosks take both coins or telephone cards. Most of Thailand is covered by mobile phone GSM or PCM networks. Internet outlets are becoming increasingly available.

Time Difference

Thailand is seven hours ahead of Greenwich Mean Time (GMT + 7).

Electricity

The electric current is 220 Volt AC 950 cycles throughout the country. A plug adaptor kit is advised. Better hotels can provide 110 volt transformers.

Weights and Measures

Thailand uses the metric system, i.e. metres and kilos in shops and kilometres on roads. Golf courses, however, are measured in yards.

Health Services

All main tourist destinations and provincial cities have hospitals and clinics with well-trained staff. Visitors should take out medical insurance before travelling because all medical treatment is chargeable. An ambulance can be called from any private hospital. Pharmacies are everywhere and will sell any required medicines without a prescription.

Useful Numbers

Tourist Assistance Centre: (02) 694 1460
Tourist Police Division: (02) 678 6800
Tourist Police Division Hotline: 1699
Tourist Service Centre: 1155
Tourist Info Service: (02) 694 1360 or (02) 694 1200 ext. 1000-5
Telephone number enquiry: 113

NATIONAL HOLIDAYS AND FESTIVALS

January 1	New Year's Day
February Full Moon Day	Magha Puja
April 6	Chakri Day
April 12-14	Songkran
May 5	Coronation Day
May Full Moon Day	Visakha Puja
July Full Moon Day	Asalha Puja
August 12	HM The Queen's Birthday
October 23	Chulalongkorn Day
November Full Moon Day	Loi Krathong
December 5	HM The King's Birthday
December 10	Constitution Day
December 31	New Year's Eve

Thailand's Best 18 Holes

It seemed an interesting idea to create a 'dream course' by selecting holes from all over Thailand. Each had to be correctly numbered and characteristic of its course, with only one hole allowed from each. This is my personal selection; I have played them all and recommend them for their design quality and golfing pedigree. Play them yourself and see if you agree. If nothing else, you will have played on 18 of Thailand's top golf courses – truly representative and arguably among the best – and, I trust, had much pleasure while doing so.

THAILAND'S BEST 18 HOLES

HOLE	YD	M	PAR	HOLE	YD	M	PAR
1	433	396	4	10	374	342	4
2	533	487	5	11	585	535	5
3	555	507	5	12	372	340	4
4	382	349	4	13	422	386	4
5	222	203	3	14	194	177	3
6	445	407	4	15	584	534	5
7	405	370	4	16	362	331	4
8	199	182	3	17	178	163	3
9	383	350	4	18	566	517	5
OUT	3557	3251	36	IN	3637	3325	37

7194YD 6576M PAR 73

Bangpra
1st hole 433yd/396m par 4

This is an intimidating opener – ranked stroke 3 on the card – played between mature trees to a slightly downhill fairway turning right and uphill to the distant green. The temptation is to overhit, but with substantial fairway bunkers lurking either side, plus a large tree, the line is narrower than it looks. The elevated green, protected by three bunkers, slopes right to left.

Laem Chabang
2nd hole 533yd/487m par 5

With water to be crossed twice, a choice must be made about position off the tee to reach the green in two. Otherwise, a safe drive over water to the right of the narrow fairway leaves a steady second across the water to a further fairway and elevated green. A vast bunker guards the front right, as does the water; too far left finds mounds or out-of-bounds.

Natural Park Hill
3rd hole 555yd/507m par 5

A fine hole that tends to deceive by an apparent innocence, but finally reveals a sting in the tail. The drive is straight downhill between tall palms. The second is similar, although the fairway narrows between mounds and palm trees. The next shot sorts the men from the boys. It plays over rock-strewn water to an uphill, well-elevated green protected by

1st hole, Bangpra

4th hole, Bangsai

three deep bunkers in front, a sprinkling of trees left and water on both sides. (See p.59.)

Bangsai
4th hole 382yd/349m par 4
This dogleg left along a valley edged with large sand dunes is not overlong, but tougher than it appears. A moderate drive enters dead ground, with no view of the green; the ideal line is long and left over the sand, but risky. The small green, protected by water and sand, requires an accurate approach. Its raised, open front and swale invites a pitch and run.

Soi Dao Highland
5th hole 223yd/203m par 3
This deceptive hole is played across a tree-filled deep depression, rushes and water, hardly visible from the tee, to an open green protected by a single bunker in front. With the green seemingly below you (it isn't) and majestic Soi Dao mountain rising behind, it appears nearer than it is. There is plenty of room short, left and right, but no easy pitch to follow to a sloping, elevated green.

Navatanee
6th hole 445yd/407m par 4
Water runs all along the left side of the hole, which slopes naturally towards it. It then cuts back across the fairway, leaving a strip of further fairway left and a long approach that is all carry over water to an uphill green ringed by bunkers. Mounds catch the safe drive right, leaving a sloping lie, and even if long and well placed, the second shot demands the utmost respect. (See p.41.)

Dragon Hills
7th hole 405yd/370m par 4
The fairway is in effect a raised plateau, slightly dogleg right, with large mounds and swales on the left and a long bunker down the right flank. The challenge, assuming a straight drive in play, lies in the second shot. Two large bunkers wait in front of the wide but very shallow raised green, with a further pot bunker centre rear. Anything a touch right falls away downhill to a deep swale.

Dynasty
8th hole 199yd/182m par 3
This hole, currently the 15th, is a strong hole carrying over a water hazard twice, with a promontory in between. The green has a vertical stone face rising from the lake and two bunkers left rear. There is plenty of room to play safely left, but if the flag is back right on this raised, angled green, it is highly challenging. The intermediate tongue of fairway foreshortens the hole.

5th hole, Soi Dao Highland

8th hole, Dynasty

Noble Place
9th hole 383yd/350m par 4

A classic dogleg left, not long, but requiring placement and accuracy. The drive is across a rocky creek. You need to avoid pairs of bunkers either side of the undulating fairway, where mounds, humps and hollows leave sloping lies. The uphill approach must clear two large bunkers deceptively short of the green and avoid further sand just left. There are large mounds behind. (See p.63).

The Majestic Creek
10th hole 374yd/342m par 4

A matter of risk and reward, with the green on this sharp, dogleg left hole open to the really long, bold hitter. However, it is all carry over water from the tee and, with the fairway barely above the water level, distance judgement is difficult. A large bunker on the far side of the fairway worries average drivers, while sand short and right of the elevated, tilted green lies in wait for the under-hit approach.

The Rose Garden
11th hole 585yd/535m par 5

One of four excellent par 5s, the hole curves continuously left, with a creek and tall trees inside. There is nothing to see off the tee, very level with a tree and bunker on the corner and a large water hazard beyond a copse right. Subtle fairway mounding can give a sloping stance, bunkers that are barely visible lie straight ahead, and trees, rocks and a lake protect the bunkered, elevated left-hand green. Treat with care.

Chiangmai-Lamphun
12th hole 372yd/340m par 4

This is a left-hand dogleg with hidden dangers lying in wait for the unwary or the careless. A winding creek, which hugs the left side from tee to green, becomes an unseen lake cutting into the fairway. It also snakes across the driving line to pass behind three right-hand fairway bunkers. Avoid these, and the approach shot is downhill across sand to a small, severely sloping green with more bunkers behind, plus the ever-present creek.

Springfield Royal
13th hole 422yd/386m par 4

This is a great hole that is typical of the designer's style. The fairway curves around a lake on the right-hand side, with a vast waste bunker between fairway and water running virtually the entire length of the hole. Just before the green, the water cuts across, demanding a high carry to a kidney-shaped target, which slopes steeply back to front and is protected by three bunkers in front and palm trees behind.

11th hole, The Rose Garden

14th hole, Blue Canyon (Canyon)

Blue Canyon (Canyon)
14th hole 194yd/177m par 3

This is a spectacular hole, with the extremely elevated tee perched high up on the canyon rim near the clubhouse/hotel. The teardrop-shaped green floating out in the lake is not as small as it looks and needs perhaps two clubs less, such is the drop. The green is 34yd/31m deep on the right, but narrows down sharply to the left. Check the pin position and any crosswind carefully. Having done so, then trust your swing. Breathtaking.

 Royal Chiangmai
15th hole 584yd/534m par 5

This is a tree-lined hole, long and uphill with a wide fairway for the tee-shot, which carries over water. Concealed water also eats into the fairway from the left further on, narrowing the target between trees. Two pairs of bunkers challenge the approach, but are deceptively short of the shallow, rising green, which is further protected by a large tree on the right. Take more club than you think.

 Royal Ratchaburi
16th hole 362yd/331m par 4

Very scenic, this severely doglegged hole offers a challenging choice. For the very bold, there is a direct line across water to a peninsula of fairway narrowed by water on both sides, sand and trees, leaving a short pitch across the lake. The alternative for the rest of us is a safer route out to the right that skirts a cluster of fairway bunkers to an angled green backed by a necklace of sand and a tree-lined slope (see p.9)

 Thai Muang Beach
17th hole 178yd/163m par 3

Known as 'The Lady', this demanding hole lies at the end of a narrowing peninsula of land set at an acute angle across water from the tee. Shored up with the signature railway sleepers, the elevated green is further protected by a long bunker in front and further water immediately behind. There is plenty of space to bail out right for a pitch in, but no room for error if you go for the flag.

 Santiburi
18th hole 566yd/517m par 5

The ideal finishing hole, a double-dogleg offering a player the chance of par for three well-executed shots but demanding perfection for two-on. The drive must avoid water along the left, which then cuts across to form a right-hand lake all the way to the green, with the tilting fairway curving towards the water, a series of bunkers and a deep swale before the two-level, bunkered putting surface.

17th hole, Thai Muang Beach

18th hole, Santiburi

Chapter 1

Bangkok and Central Plains

Bangkok, or Krungthep, the 'City of Angels', is a city of contrasts. In keeping with the basic Thai nature of relaxed tolerance, ancient and modern happily coexist side by side. This sprawling metropolis (it covers 1567 sq km/605 sq miles) has some of the world's most beautiful temples and ancient Buddhist shrines. It also has an emerging downtown skyline of high-rise skyscrapers, the elevated Skytrain and some of world's worst traffic jams, along with the inevitable noise and pollution. Bangkok is a renowned location for shopping and dining out. It is also the world's hottest capital city. The average temperature is 36°C; it rarely goes below 25°C, and, from March to May, can creep up to 42°C.

Left: The chedi, library *and* prang *of Prasat Phra Thep Bidom, Wat Phra Keo at the Grand Palace.*
Above: Richly exotic – Thai orchids.

Situated in the centre of the country, the middle of Thailand's agricultural rice bowl, Bangkok is the main gateway for all visitors and their first venture into the intriguing and attractive cultural mix that is Thailand. The city is home to some 8 million people, which is around 13 per cent of the national population, and roughly half of them are of Chinese descent. Bangkok was founded in 1782 by King Rama I, who decided to move the capital east across the Chao Phraya River from Thonburi. This 'River of Kings', which winds through the modern city in the same manner as the Thames in London or the Seine in Paris, was the source for the many canals or *khlongs* which, until the mid-19th century, provided the only means of access and transport throughout the capital. The lack of any roads suitable for wheeled vehicles led to the city being called the 'Venice of the Orient'. Most of these canals have now been filled in, but a few can still be found in Thonburi, just across from a loop in the river known as Ratanakosin Island, where the main royal buildings and temples are located.

Golf in Thailand offers world-class facilities with added local colour. But, golf visitors will also enjoy sightseeing, shopping, cultural activities and dining. In Bangkok, this means taking time to admire the entrancing confluence of religion, history and ethnic creativity in the royal palaces, temples (*wats*) and other notable buildings – timeless beauty that no amount of modern infrastructure can replace.

Top of every visitor's list is the Grand Palace and Wat Phra Keo. They are part of

Below: Performed in elegant ancient costume, Thai classical dance transcends time.

a compound on Ratanakosin Island comprising more than 100 buildings reflecting over 200 years of Thai royal history. Wat Phra Keo houses the Emerald Buddha, the most sacred image in the kingdom. The 75-cm/30-in high statue, set up high in a golden sanctuary, has its jewelled costume ceremoniously changed by the king to mark each of the three seasons. Nearby is Wat Pho, which is the oldest and largest temple in Bangkok. This houses the famous Reclining Buddha, which is 46m (50yd) long and covered in gold leaf.

Bangkok's heart lies in its main waterway, and a lunch or dinner cruise along the Chao Phraya provides a rewarding perspective on Bangkok life. It also offers fine views of Wat Arun, the Temple of the Dawn, with its main central *prang* towering up 104m (341ft). Its dazzling surface, best seen from the Bangkok shore at sunset, is made up of countless porcelain fragments, originally used as ballast by visiting Chinese traders. Another popular spot that is in the same area is Wat Saket and the Golden Mount, which rewards those who make the climb with a stunning view of the surroundings.

Slightly further north, the Dusit area contains the current royal residence, the Chitralada Palace and the Vimanmek Palace, favoured by King Rama V. This is the world's largest mansion built of golden teak wood, without a single nail, and it is full of interesting artefacts and period atmosphere. A taxi to the Yaowarat Road area brings you to the narrow, winding alleys (*sois*) of old Chinatown. This is the site of Wat Traimit, the Temple of the Golden Buddha, which is 3m (10ft) high and made of solid gold weighing 5.5 tonnes.

For antique domestic charm, visit Jim

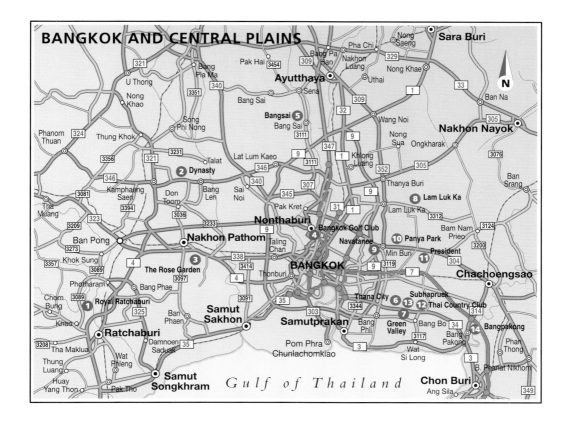

Thomson's house. The man who restored the silk industry after World War II, and later disappeared in mysterious circumstances, left behind a traditional Thai-style house and a priceless collection of Oriental antiques.

Bangkok has a deserved reputation as a shopper's paradise. Whether in modern shopping plazas or on market stalls, one can discover great bargains in fashion, silk, hand-embroidered goods, gems, jewellery, art and antiques. In department stores, you pay the stated price but elsewhere enjoy the expected practice of bargaining, which may save you as much as 30 per cent. The weekend Chatuchak market is a vast open-air affair selling virtually anything, while a visit to legendary Patpong Road is an experience in itself.

Its reputation for sexy nightlife has been rather superseded by some good restaurants and crowded night-time market stalls. These are noted for offering cheap copies of leading international brands, from watches to luggage. As for dining, the choice city-wide is truly international and reflects the Thai penchant for eating out.

Not too far out of the city, there are a number of locations for interesting day excursions. Just to the north is the ancient Siamese capital of Ayutthaya, founded in 1350. To the west, discover the floating market at Damnoen Saduak (see photo p.108) and the eclectic daily cultural show at The Rose Garden. There is also the great *chedi* at Nakhon Pathom, the tallest Buddhist structure in the world.

Royal Ratchaburi

*Royal Ratchaburi Golf Club, Khao Rank, Amphur
Muang, Ratchaburi 70000*
TEL: *(032) 321 061* **FAX:** *(032) 321 061*
LOCATION: *8km NW of Ratchaburi city; Route
3087/Route 3089 via Route 4*
COURSE: *18 holes, 6785yd/6204m, par 72*
TYPE OF COURSE: *Undulating, well-bunkered
parkland course embracing the lower slopes of a forested
mountain*
DESIGNER: *Artanan Yomchinda (1988)*
GREEN FEES: *B*
FACILITIES: *Golf shop, caddies, cart and golf equipment
hire, shoe and umbrella rental, driving range, putting
green, changing facilities, swimming pool, tennis court,
refreshment shelters on course, restaurant in clubhouse*
VISITORS: *Welcome, but telephone in advance*

ROYAL RATCHABURI

HOLE	YD	M	PAR	HOLE	YD	M	PAR
1	497	454	5	10	369	337	4
2	198	181	3	11	161	147	3
3	454	415	4	12	470	430	4
4	404	369	4	13	527	482	5
5	390	357	4	14	428	391	4
6	380	347	4	15	196	179	3
7	142	130	3	16	362	331	4
8	387	354	4	17	550	503	5
9	525	480	5	18	345	315	4
OUT	3377	3088	36	IN	3408	3116	36

6785YD • 6204M • PAR 72

This course is an excellent introduction to the wealth and variety of golf in Thailand. About a 90-minute drive west of central Bangkok, it is set in gently rolling parkland at the base of wooded mountains. Essentially a members' club, it offers a friendly welcome to visitors.

It is the two main mountains – Khao Rang and Khao Chonglao – that make this course. They not only separate the two nines, with their dense vegetation and rocky crags providing a dramatic backdrop, but influence the lie of the land. Many holes hug the surrounding slopes before easing down to some fine strategic tests across and around a number of lakes. Well established, with a fine selection of mature trees, the course is kept in excellent condition.

This is a real pleasure to play, with its not-too-demanding fairways – some split-level – rolling, plunging and rising past bright splashes of colour, a good variety of trees and gentle mounding at the sides to well-protected greens. The lake holes, which are a part of both nines, feature large areas of sand, rocks and deep greenside traps. They contrast with the mountain holes, naturally shaped by the land, with some steeply sloping greens to match. There is a certain amount of movement and roll in the fairways, but it is not too severe. As the rough is fairly dense, however, it pays to play conservatively on what is not an overlong layout, while the fairway bunkers are set deeply enough below the mounds to restrict any long recovery.

On the front nine, the 6th is a very attractive medium par 4, with the approach to the green over a right-hand rock-encircled lake plus three bunkers, with six more ringing the green behind. The following hole is short, but to an island green, where accurate clubbing is essential. The 9th, par 5, doglegs right out of a narrow chute, gently uphill to a small, elevated green protected by a deep bunker right.

The finishing holes are memorable, and not just because of the views. The sharply doglegged left 16th fairway divides around a lake, with a narrow, direct line to the green for the bold and a safer route right for the rest of us (see photo p.9). The par 5 17th curves the other way uphill, offering beautiful mountain views and a steep, difficult green protected by no less than 10 bunkers. Local, ball-hungry monkeys lurk near the 18th tee, which plays, on different days, to two quite

Above: The 10th hole is not long, but the green is well defended by a single tree and much sand.

different greens – one straightforward and the other tucked round right across a rocky water hazard at the base of the mountain.

There is a 19th hole, with bunkers and chipping green on the site of the planned clubhouse. The temporary clubhouse is open, airy, with friendly, quite adequate service and facilities. Well worth the trip.

Below: The approach at the par 4 6th must carry water, rocks and a tight protective ring of bunkers.

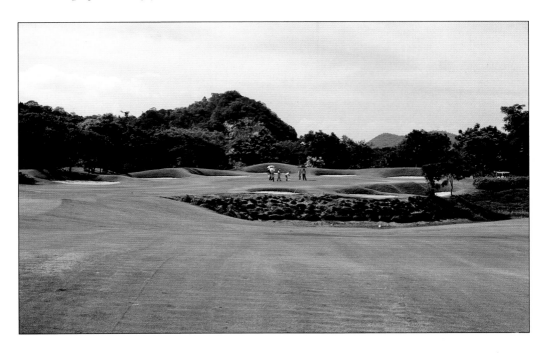

Dynasty

Dynasty Golf & Country Club, 99 Moo 3, Poldumri Road, Banglen, Nakhon Pathom 73130
TEL: *(034) 391 076-9, (034) 391 333* **FAX:** *(034) 391 111*
LOCATION: *Km 58 marker Route 346 via Routes 3036 and 4*
COURSE: *18 holes, 6780yd/6200m, par 72*
TYPE OF COURSE: *Gently undulating parkland with many strategic water hazards*
DESIGNER: *Dennis Griffiths (1994)*
GREEN FEES: *B*
FACILITIES: *Golf shop, caddies, cart and golf equipment hire, shoe and umbrella rental, driving range, putting green, changing facilities, refreshment shelters on course, restaurant in clubhouse*
VISITORS: *Welcome, but telephone in advance*

DYNASTY							
HOLE	YD	M	PAR	HOLE	YD	M	PAR
1	410	375	4	10	520	475	5
2	380	347	4	11	461	421	4
3	368	336	4	12	185	169	3
4	382	349	4	13	389	356	4
5	522	477	5	14	363	332	4
6	154	141	3	15	199	182	3
7	542	496	5	16	478	437	5
8	447	409	4	17	411	376	4
9	185	169	3	18	396	362	4
OUT	3390	3100	36	IN	3390	3100	36

6780YD • 6200M • PAR 72

The downturn in Thailand's economy a few years ago, which followed hard on the heels of a massive explosion in golf course construction, left many entrepreneurs and land developers with serious financial problems. However, this unfortunate state of affairs has proved to be a bonus for the visiting player. In the euphoric early 1990s, grand plans involved building international specification golf courses, mostly designed by world-famous golf-course architects. To attract investors, the golf course was the first item to be finished, usually to the highest standards. Other plans may have gone on hold, but these courses remain. They offer a wealth of top-class golfing challenges, are kept in excellent condition and are on offer at rock-bottom prices. Holiday golfers have never had it so good.

Dynasty Golf and Country Club, just a short drive north-west from Bangkok, is a typical example. Planned as an urban village within commuting distance of the metropolis, the master plan incorporated 27 holes of golf on level land. Considerable earthmoving was required to raise the course above the water table and a sophisticated drainage and irrigation system installed. The original plan also offered a grand clubhouse, tennis, badminton, swimming and watersports as well as the sale of a large number of integrated building plots, mostly golf-facing, to house

Above: Players approaching the seriously challenging par 3 15th (see also p.19).

the members. Only 18 holes have been completed so far, along with a temporary clubhouse. This is warm and welcoming, however, and provides just the right atmosphere for a golfer's club.

The excellent course was designed by Dennis Griffiths, whose other notable efforts in Thailand include the Thai Country Club and Soi Dao Highland. The high level of maintenance enhances a very peaceful location. It is an ideal setting for a day's golf, not too far from the capital and well manicured, all for a nominal weekday green fee of 400 baht (250 baht on Wednesdays and Fridays)!

Due to the current location of the clubhouse, the course starts at what will be the 18th and follows an eclectic path before finishing on what should be the 11th. Water, ever-present along the sloping edges of all the

holes but one, forms an attractive framework to the course, as do plenty of mature trees. The par 3s are excellent (see p.19). This is a very natural design with gentle mounding and shallow swales, plus some transverse water at strategic distances. The course is beautifully kept with flowering shrubs, little hedges, flame trees and palms. Relaxing, interesting golf at a bargain price – who could ask for more?

SIAMESE SPORT

Sanuk (having fun) takes many forms. In the hottest months, kite fighting is a popular pastime. Giant *chula* (or male) kites try to snare a smaller *pukpao* (or female) kite to their territory. The latter, which are more agile, try to loop their lines around the *chulas*, bringing them down to their level. Another pastime, which has developed into a legitimate sport, is *takraw*. This involves keeping a light rattan ball in the air as long as possible, using feet, knees, elbows and head but not hands.

The Rose Garden

The Rose Garden Golf Course, Km 32, Pet Kasem
Highway, Sampran, Nakhon Pathom 73110
TEL: (034) 322 544-7; 225 202-6 **FAX:** (034) 322
775
LOCATION: 32km west of Bangkok by Route 4
COURSE: 18 holes, 7085yd/6478m, par 72
TYPE OF COURSE: Well-established level parkland
with mature trees and a number of strategic water hazards
DESIGNER: Visudh Junnanont (1972)
GREEN FEES: BB
FACILITIES: Golf shop, caddies, cart and golf equipment
hire, driving range, putting green, changing facilities, own
hotel with swimming pool nearby, refreshment shelters on
course, restaurants in clubhouse
VISITORS: Welcome, but advance booking necessary.
Closed Mondays

THE ROSE GARDEN

HOLE	YD	M	PAR	HOLE	YD	M	PAR
1	355	325	4	10	365	334	4
2	440	402	4	11	585	535	5
3	360	329	4	12	400	366	4
4	210	192	3	13	365	334	4
5	555	507	5	14	160	146	3
6	180	165	3	15	205	187	3
7	555	507	5	16	445	407	4
8	420	384	4	17	445	407	4
9	450	411	4	18	590	539	5
OUT	3525	3223	36	IN	3560	3255	36

7085YD • 6478M • PAR 72

This course, part of a delightful tourist
resort some 40 minutes west of Bangkok,
was among the first of what could be termed
the 'modern era' of golf course construction
in Thailand. Designed as a true visitor facility,
rather than an upmarket membership club
linked to real estate development, it has
withstood the test of time and still deserves its
place among the most popular tourist
locations. This reflects well
on the enlightened
management and the

continuing care and improvement made by
the Thai designer, Visudh Junnanont. The
Rose Garden remains unique in its personal
approach, considerable charm, attention to
detail and determination that every visitor
should enjoy being there.

The name derives from the creation, in the
early 1960s, of a floral garden by the owning
family, which developed into a commercial
success. This in turn led to the creation,
innovative at that time, of a tourist resort.
Increasing popularity saw the introduction of a
range of visitor facilities, including a daily
cultural show, manicured gardens, a hotel and
the 18-hole golf course. The personal touch
remains at the core of The Rose Garden's
attraction, although the 'family' now
includes more than 1000 employees.

Originally constructed from rice
paddy and swampland, the course
occupies 175 acres/700 sq km of
essentially level terrain. However,
the many palm and other trees have
matured to define
each   hole,

supplemented by colourful flowers and shrubs – flame red, purple, white and yellow – plus lotus in the many water hazards. Considerable shaping and gentle mounding has been introduced over the years to raise and accentuate the well-conditioned fairways. Each hole has two slightly elevated greens, ensuring continuous play, regular maintenance and some strategic variety.

This course, which has hosted the Thailand Open in the past, is an excellent test of golf. The most memorable holes are almost certainly the par 5s. The 5th has an angled creek to carry from the tee and a narrowing fairway towards the green. This is followed by the 7th, played over and between water up a tight, mounded fairway to an elevated, offset green (see photo p.1). On the back nine, the 11th requires careful placement round a severe left-hand dogleg with a water carry to the green, while the final hole demands a

Above: Colourful flowers are a feature of this course – here they are seen framing the 10th tee.

good drive and an accurate approach over water and rocks to a tilted, elevated target.

Playing here is an experience to cherish. Features include peacocks, red-necked cranes and the expert caddies in red straw hats. There are subtle swales, humps and hollows and deceptive lengths; 'khlong' boys in the water hazards who retrieve your errant shot for 5 baht; iced water on a silver tray after the ninth green; and a chilled towel when you finish. The level of service is worth the visit alone.

Below: The approach to the water-protected 18th green with the fine modern clubhouse in the background.

Bangkok Golf Club

Bangkok Golf Club, 99 Moo 2, Tiwanon Road, Bangkadi, Pathumthani 12000
TEL: *(02) 501 2828* **FAX:** *(02) 501 2810*
EMAIL: *bkgolf@ksc.th.com*
LOCATION: *West Bangkok suburbs, 20 minutes from Don Muang airport. Route 306 via Routes 1 and 31*
COURSE: *18 holes, 6918yd/6326m, par 72; also 9 holes par 27*
TYPE OF COURSE: *Compact, urban parkland layout of quality with many strategic hazards*
DESIGNER: *Chird Boonyaratanavej (1993)*
GREEN FEES: *BBB*
FACILITIES: *Golf shop, caddies, cart and golf equipment hire, umbrella and shoe rental, driving range, putting greens, changing facilities, Thai massage, refreshment shelters on course, restaurants in clubhouse*
VISITORS: *Welcome, but telephone in advance*

BANGKOK GOLF CLUB

HOLE	YD	M	PAR	HOLE	YD	M	PAR
1	381	348	4	10	357	326	4
2	175	160	3	11	196	179	3
3	368	336	4	12	535	489	5
4	591	540	5	13	427	390	4
5	168	154	3	14	201	184	3
6	378	346	4	15	420	384	4
7	419	383	4	16	365	334	4
8	612	560	5	17	401	367	4
9	372	340	4	18	552	505	5
OUT	3464	3167	36	IN	3454	3158	36

6918YD • 6326M • PAR 72

Close to town (20 minutes from the airport and 30 minutes from the city centre) and cleverly laid out by a relatively unknown Thai architect on a neat and compact site, this course provides highly strategic golf in immaculately manicured condition. This is essentially a well-appointed members' club, although visitors can play with advance booking.

well as a good touch on the excellent greens. It is difficult to avoid the urban landscape outside the course, despite the many trees and flowering shrubs that are fast maturing, but every effort has been made to create an atmosphere of beauty within. There are exotic species of wildfowl, colourful flowers, and even a spectacular waterfall edging the elevated par 5 8th green after a carry over water. The fairways have gentle slopes and the bunkers are mostly shallow. The caddies know the course well and everything is maintained in superb condition to ensure the player's enjoyment.

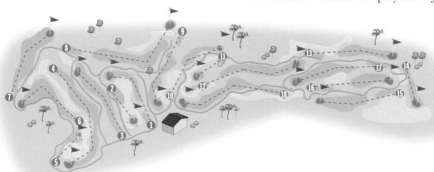

Despite occupying a comparatively small area of suburban land, the course stretches to nearly 7000yd (6400m) from the back tees and, with a number of water hazards affecting play on nearly every hole, proves an exacting test. Accuracy is the key ingredient here as

The club has hosted a number of important tournaments, both amateur and professional, including the Thailand Ladies Open between 1999 and 2001 (an event, incidentally, pioneered by the author in 1984). A worldwide poll of the best 500 holes in the world in 2000 by the American *Golf*

Above: There is much to distract the player's eye on the approach to the 8th green, including this spectacular water feature.

Magazine, chose Bangkok Golf Club's 18th as one of five in Thailand. A double-dogleg par 5 of 552yd/505m, it makes a genuinely exciting finishing hole. Each shot requires great care and placement to avoid water and sand, which narrow its sinuous fairway on both sides before demanding an approach across water to a relatively small, sloping green.

In addition to an excellent floodlit driving range and other practice facilities, the club boasts a novel nine-hole par 3 course, open to the public and floodlit at night. The holes (particularly the greens) are each modelled after famous short holes around the world. You can play the 8th at Royal Troon, the 7th at Pebble

Below: The unique par 3 course offers a worldwide championship tour.

Beach, even the notorious 12th at Augusta, without leaving Bangkok. Soft spikes are required on the immaculate playing surfaces.

The clubhouse has an excellent pro-shop and three restaurants – Vino Rosso for Italian fare and grills, Akamon for Japanese cuisine with a view and Fairways, which serves Thai, Chinese and European choices. A 78-bedroom spa resort on the property opened in 2001, offering accommodation and treatments for both members and guests.

Bangsai Country Club

Bangsai Country Club, 77/7 Moo 3, Bangplee,
Bangsai, Ayutthaya 13190
TEL: *(035) 371 490-7* **FAX:** *(035) 371 491*
EMAIL: *bangsaicc@hotmail.com*
LOCATION: *Km 22 marker, Route 3111 via Routes*
346 and 1
COURSE: *18 holes, 6923yd/6330m, par 72*
TYPE OF COURSE: *Gently undulating course offering*
variety of parkland and links-style holes with strategic
water
DESIGNER: *Pirapon Namatra (1996)*
GREEN FEES: *B*
FACILITIES: *Golf shop, caddies, cart and golf equipment*
hire, umbrella and shoe rental, driving range, putting
green, changing facilities, refreshment shelters on course,
restaurant in clubhouse
VISITORS: *Welcome, but telephone in advance*

BANGSAI COUNTRY CLUB

HOLE	YD	M	PAR	HOLE	YD	M	PAR
1	446	407	4	10	546	500	5
2	304	277	4	11	453	414	4
3	541	495	5	12	177	162	3
4	382	349	4	13	425	389	4
5	390	357	4	14	584	534	5
6	221	202	3	15	418	382	4
7	375	343	4	16	206	188	3
8	164	150	3	17	352	322	4
9	503	460	5	18	436	399	4
OUT	3326	3041	36	IN	3597	3289	36

6923YD • 6330M • PAR 72

It is a rare but exhilarating experience to discover an outstanding golf course that is a first design effort by an amateur. The course at Bangsai, near the historic ancient city of Ayutthaya, is one to savour and deserves better recognition.

Given that it started life as a totally flat rice field, this is a real gem, created with great imagination and flair. The owner's son, an American-educated Thai in his early twenties and a good player, set out to create a course offering genuine variety, with each hole presenting a different challenge – a course that would be interesting for members and visitors alike. He studied the work of great architects of the past, such as Dr Alistair McKenzie, in the use of dead ground to deceive the eye. He also tried to recreate varying playing conditions, such as having an area of 'seaside links holes complete with sand dunes'. The site is cleverly contained within dykes

to prevent flooding. Every aspect of the design, including every bunker, had to receive paternal approval. The result is a pleasure to behold and a delight to play.

Given the exposed nature of the rural locale and the opportunities for a cooling breeze, the deliberate attempt to create a seaside feel is a master stroke. Four holes, from the 3rd to the 6th, wind through an area of bare sand dunes and tussocks of lemongrass – links golf in the tropics. Others flow and undulate past waste bunkers with plenty of fairway movement, little humps and hollows, many sloping lies, and peninsulas of low rough mounds that creep out into fairways

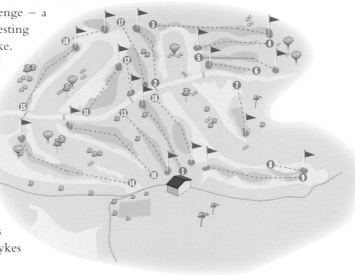

snaking sinuously past. With greens edged by grassy swales and pot bunkers offering an open foregreen for the pitch and run, Scotland is here at last.

Apart from the challenge of the 4th hole (see p.18), some of the most memorable holes are the shortest. The tees at the 6th, 221yd/202m, are set on a series of staggered mounds, played across a rippled valley with bunkers right to a long, uphill, kidney-shaped green. If a par 3 can ever be dogleg left, this is it. The short 12th, 177yd/162m, is full of seaside character. It demands a high carry to a shallow, angled, elevated green across two large bunkers with another back left. At 206yd/188m, the 16th is really testing. Played across water to an uphill sloping green protected by five bunkers, which start some 70 yards from the putting surface, it presents an inviting target angled towards the water

Below: The uphill sloping par 3 16th demands a long, precise shot to avoid the sand and water.

right. Like the 4th, the 17th rewards a long drive with a level plateau of fairway. Anything short is uphill and blind to the green. This shortish four is made by the approach. Twin palms mask the centre of a seriously humpbacked, shallow green, which has a grass pot bunker and deep swale in front and a severe downhill slope behind.

All in all, this is a real golfer's course, with enough trees and water to keep you honest and a good variety of tees to suit all levels.

In keeping with the concept of the course, the part-timbered clubhouse is relaxed and unassuming, conveying the traditional charm of a golf club. The comfortable, welcoming restaurant, which offers a library of golf magazines, is at ground level, with either air-conditioned or covered terrace tables, the latter leading directly out onto the course. Pleasantly unpretentious in all aspects, with service to match, Bangsai is a treat for any golfer. Underplayed and undervalued, it is a real gem, currently at bargain rates.

6 Thana City

*Thana City Golf & Country Club, 100–100/1 Moo
4, Bangna–Trad Highway, Km 14, Bangchalong,
Bangplee, Samutprakarn 10540*
TEL: *(02) 336 1968-74* **FAX:** *(02) 336 1979-80*
EMAIL: *thanacty@loxinfo.co.th*
LOCATION: *20 minutes from Sukhumvit Road, at Km
14 on Route 34*
COURSE: *18 holes, 6966yd/6370m, par 72*
TYPE OF COURSE: *A cross between links and heath
over level land*
DESIGNER: *Greg Norman (1993)*
GREEN FEES: *BBB/BBBB after 0930 Wed-Fri*
FACILITIES: *Pro shop, caddies, cart and golf equipment
hire, shoe, chair and umbrella rental, driving range,
putting green, changing facilities, refreshment shelters on
course, restaurant in clubhouse, sports complex with
fitness centre, tennis courts, gymnasium, Olympic-size
swimming pool, sauna and Jacuzzi*
VISITORS: *Visitors welcome, but advance booking
recommended*

Planned as a satellite commuter township
just south-east of Bangkok along the super
highway, Thana City lies on a very level site
punctuated by skyscraper condominium
blocks. The golf clubhouse dominates one side
of the course, the high-rises another two. In
between, Greg Norman has created something
of a hybrid layout. Some holes are reminiscent
of the seaside links in Britain that he knows
and admires. Other holes resemble windswept
heathland, while many of the greens, edging
water, have the jigsaw-shaped bunkers edged
with railway sleepers found in Florida.

A lack of trees has been compensated for
with clumps of coarse grass, reeds, sand and
gentle, subtly undulating fairways open to the
breeze. There are only moderate amounts of
strategic water and all is clearly visible. This is
a very definite test, short of floral dressing but
long on shotmaking and club judgement,
with one or two heroic carries for par.

The restaurant offers Thai, Western,
Japanese and Chinese cuisine along with a
fine golfing view.

*Below: The 9th and 18th greens finish right in front of the
imposing clubhouse complex.*

7 Green Valley

*Green Valley Country Club, 92 Moo 3, Km 15
Bangna–Trad Highway, Bangplee, Samutprakarn
10540*
TEL: *(02) 312 5883-89* **FAX:** *(02) 312 5890*
EMAIL: *komjakra@kscll.th.com*
LOCATION: *Near Km 15 on Route 34 south-west
from Bangkok*
COURSE: *18 holes, 7028yd/6426m, par 72*
TYPE OF COURSE: *Mature level parkland with much
strategic water*
DESIGNER: *Robert Trent Jones Jr (1988)*
GREEN FEES: *BBBB*
FACILITIES: *Golf shop, caddies, cart and golf equipment
hire, shoe and umbrella rental, driving range, putting
green, changing facilities, sauna, massage, swimming
pool, refreshment shelters on course, restaurant in
clubhouse*
VISITORS: *Advance booking necessary; soft spikes
required*

This is one of the earlier of the new breed
of members' clubs built around Bangkok
and is starting to show its age a little. On the
bonus side, the trees and course have matured
well and all is kept in good condition. This is
very much a members' club, rather than a
commercial operation. Although visitors are
welcome if booked in advance, the green fee
is quite steep by Thai standards.

The course is typical of the work of
Robert Trent Jones Jr. It is fairly gentle for
the members off their preferred tee but tough
off the back, following the philosophy
propounded by Robert Trent Jones Sr of
'easy bogey, difficult par'.

This is a player's course, quite long, with
water eating into some fairways and across the
front of the greens. It is a genuine challenge
for middle- to low-handicappers. There are
rippling, gently mounded fairways bordered
by larger mounds and trees, plus plenty of
flowers and highly strategic water. The best
hole could well be the par 3 12th, 206yd/
188m from the back, carrying water all the
way to the flag if you are brave enough.

*Below: The course and clubhouse are backed by many lush
and well-established trees.*

8 *Lam Luk Ka*

*Lam Luk Ka Country Club, 29 Moo 7, Tambol Lam
Sai, Lam Lukka (Klong 11), Pathumthani 12150*
TEL: *(02) 995 2300-4* **FAX:** *(02) 995 2305*
EMAIL: *lvlk@asianet.co.th*
LOCATION: *Off Route 305 at Km 27 marker*
COURSE: *36 holes: East Course 7012yd/6412m;
West Course 6605yd/6040m, both par 72*
TYPE OF COURSE: *Well-contoured 36-hole parkland
layout elevated above extensive areas of water*
DESIGNER: *Roger Packard (1994)*
GREEN FEES: *BB*
FACILITIES: *Golf shop, caddies, cart and golf equipment
hire, shoe and umbrella rental, driving range, putting
greens, changing facilities, swimming pool, refreshment
shelters on course, restaurants in clubhouse*
VISITORS: *Welcome, but advance booking necessary*

LAM LUK KA EAST COURSE

HOLE	YD	M	PAR	HOLE	YD	M	PAR
1	408	373	4	10	399	365	4
2	554	549	5	11	525	480	5
3	160	146	3	12	169	154	3
4	393	359	4	13	441	403	4
5	385	352	4	14	410	375	4
6	218	199	3	15	374	342	4
7	428	391	4	16	206	188	3
8	453	414	4	17	420	384	4
9	510	466	5	18	559	511	5
OUT	3509	3209	36	IN	3503	3203	36

7012YD • 6412M • PAR 72

LAM LUK KA WEST COURSE

HOLE	YD	M	PAR	HOLE	YD	M	PAR
1	344	315	4	10	347	317	4
2	554	506	5	11	383	350	4
3	171	156	3	12	180	164	3
4	395	361	4	13	529	484	5
5	386	353	4	14	385	352	4
6	347	317	4	15	381	348	4
7	510	466	5	16	175	160	3
8	165	151	3	17	516	472	5
9	422	386	4	18	415	379	4
OUT	3294	3012	36	IN	3311	3027	36

6605YD • 6040M • PAR 72

Another refreshing example of the work of
American Roger Packard (see pp.126-
27), this club offers 36 holes of interesting golf
on a grand scale, 27km/17 miles east of the
international airport. Planned as a real estate
venture, the four nine-hole loops radiate out
from a central clubhouse complex across the
capacious 1200-acre estate.

The course is sited on the central lowland
plain surrounding Bangkok, a totally level
region devoted to rice farming due to the high
water table. Virtually every hole on the course
is affected, often seriously, by a succession of
large lakes. To avoid any risk of flooding,
particularly in the rainy season, the architect
has raised the holes well above the water level,
creating a delightfully mounded and undulating
(if wholly artificial) world apart, with steep
slopes at the sides for any errant shots.

This is golf to suit all players; with the
choice of length' on the tougher East course
or finesse and accuracy on the shorter West.
Open since 1994 (the 36 holes were
completed in 1996), the gently rolling
fairways are lined with a range of mature
trees, tall and slender to the sides, chunky
palms behind the elevated Tifdwarf greens.
On such a large area of land, tucked away in
the countryside yet within reasonable reach of

the city, there is a genuine feeling of isolation
and peace, the perfect antidote to the frenetic
bustle and traffic of Bangkok. Given the
opportunity to design the course upwards
from a very level base, the architect has in
effect produced a piece of land sculpture.
There is continuous movement here; the
fairways roll and curve past large mounds,
deep bunkers, attractive – if highly strategic –
lakes, often edged with large rocks and hardly
a flat lie on the course, in complete contrast
to the surrounding, very level countryside.
There are no sharp edges and there is nothing
mechanical. The mounding and movement
create a most pleasant place to play.

Viewed from above, there appears to be as
much water as golf course. The holes wind

and curve in green ribbons of elevated land, often sloping down to water on both sides, interlinked by a series of attractive bridges. When the perimeter and golf-facing housing is in place, this might well be likened to an Asian Venice. With 36 holes offering continuous variety, there is much to enjoy. This is very much a matter of knowing your abilities and playing within them. There are many large areas of sand, sometimes punctuated with clumps of seagrass, much penal water to carry to elevated targets and some fairly narrow fairways. A host of friendly caddies in pale pink and light green uniforms will try to keep you in play, provided you listen, and there are reviving cold drink shelters at regular intervals. This is definitely a player's layout, demanding yet rewarding, with much to feast the eye on – colourful flowers, decorative shrubs, rock gardens, cascading waterfalls supported by the

Below: Typical features of this course – slopes, mounds, deep bunkers, rocks and a variety of colourful foliage.

THAI TABOOS

Thais revere modesty and good manners. Apart from the cultural customs in the Introduction (p.16), avoid disrespect to the monarchy or any Buddha image, pointing your feet at anyone, touching people's heads, raising your voice, having a public argument, losing your temper, dressing immodestly, touching a woman, or causing 'loss of face'. You will earn considerable respect.

continuous movement of this rolling, undulating layout.

With so much good golf to play, the club is popular with large groups, so an advance reservation is essential. The capacious clubhouse is well appointed, with good locker rooms and a sizeable pro-shop. There is an air-conditioned restaurant as well as a café alongside the outdoor free-form swimming pool. Other facilities include a large practice putting green and driving range.

9 Navatanee

Navatanee Golf Course, 22 Navatanee Road, Kannayao, Bangkok 10230
TEL: *(02) 376 1032-6, 376 1693-5* **FAX:** *(02) 376 1685*
EMAIL: *navatanee@hotmail.com*
LOCATION: *Close to Siam Park, 15 minutes from Sukhumvit on Route 3278*
COURSE: *18 holes, 6902yd/6311m, par 72*
TYPE OF COURSE: *Mature parkland course of championship calibre, venue for 1975 World Cup, recently reconstructed*
DESIGNER: *Robert Trent Jones Jr (1973 and 1997)*
GREEN FEES: *BB (with member/introduction); overseas visitors BBBBB*
FACILITIES: *Golf shop, caddies, cart (obligatory) and golf equipment hire, shoe and umbrella rental, putting green, changing facilities, sauna, tennis, swimming pool, refreshment shelters on course, restaurants in clubhouse*
VISITORS: *Advance booking necessary. Non-members may play with member in group or with introductory letter. Overseas visitors call (02) 376 1031 for arrangement at 2200 baht per person, 18 holes, weekdays only*

NAVATANEE

HOLE	YD	M	PAR	HOLE	YD	M	PAR
1	442	404	4	10	427	390	4
2	389	356	4	11	198	181	3
3	558	510	5	12	383	350	4
4	135	123	3	13	580	530	5
5	329	300	4	14	368	336	4
6	445	407	4	15	422	386	4
7	216	197	3	16	393	359	4
8	386	353	4	17	159	145	3
9	552	505	5	18	540	494	5
OUT	3432	3138	36	IN	3470	3173	36

6902YD • 6311M • PAR 72

This is one of the earliest of the country's new breed of courses, created especially as a championship test for the 1975 World Cup (won by the US team of Lou Graham and Johnny Miller). The far-sighted owner, Sukum Navapan, enlisted the help of American golf architect

presented a particular set of challenges to the designer. The perennially high water table and seasonal monsoon rain meant that the property had to be protected by dykes from the surrounding land and the individual holes of the course built up sufficiently to avoid any water problems.

With its punitive bunkering, excellent use of water on its many doglegs and relatively narrow fairways, Navatanee has always had an international championship specification. In 1997, the club decided that, to improve drainage, the course should be completely reconstructed while retaining its much-respected

Robert Trent Jones Jr to create his first course in South-East Asia – the only truly international-standard design in Thailand at that time. The original location, on flooded rice paddy fields just east of Bangkok,

design. Under the supervision of the original architect, this has now produced a genuinely classic course. It is worthy of its place in any world rankings and as demanding a test of the game as any could require (although more manageable for members from the middle tees). Backed by a wealth of mature trees, the pristine fairways now undulate gently past strategic mounds and sculpted sand. The rough is normally kept at a playable level and the manicured course is in superb condition. The American magazine *Golf Digest* recently rated the course the best in Thailand; its rival in the field, *Golf World*, placed the 6th hole in the world's top 500 and Thailand's top five.

Two great holes turn up on the front nine. The 6th, much improved over its predecessor, plays to 445yd/407m off the back tee and has water all along the left-hand side of a fairway tilting left. To the right are a series of large mounds and a fairway bunker. Play safely to the right and your second can be off a sloping uphill lie. The hole then turns left, crossing the substantial water hazard with a long carry to an uphill, sloping green well protected by sand. Even if you lay up short on this demanding par 4, you will be left with a shot of at least 150yd/137m to the putting surface. The other hole is the 9th (formerly the 18th), a 552yd/505m par 5, where a large left-hand lake runs from tee to green on this left-curving dogleg and also crosses the fairway at a crucial distance. There is a clear choice – aim left and risk the lake to leave a chance to carry over the water to be close or on the green; or play safely right in two shots and face a longer shot over water and much sand.

Navatanee is a private members' club, but such has been the interest from visitors to play that the club has found a way for foreigners to be 'introduced' weekdays only, on payment of a substantial fee (currently 2200 baht). Visit, however, and you will be treated like royalty, both in the well-appointed clubhouse and on the course. Both caddie and golf cart are obligatory; the former are some of the best turned out and able in the country.

Below: A player's view of the demanding 6th hole, where both placement and length are required.

10 *Panya Park*

Panya Park Golf Course, 46 Moo 8, Suwinthawong Road Km 9.5, Nongchok, Bangkok 10530
TEL: *(02) 989 4200-23* FAX: *(02) 989 4224-25*
LOCATION: *16 km east of Minburi on Suwinthawong Road*
COURSE: *27 holes, A 3431yd/3137m; B 3473yd/3175m; C 3497yd/3198m, all par 36*
TYPE OF COURSE: *Landscaped level parkland with well-defined sand and water hazards*
DESIGNER: *Ronald Fream (1993)*
GREEN FEES: *BBB; closed Tuesdays*
FACILITIES: *Golf shop, caddies, cart and golf equipment hire, shoe, umbrella and chair rental, driving range, putting green, changing facilities, sauna, refreshment shelters on course, restaurant in clubhouse*
VISITORS: *Welcome, but advance reservation necessary*

This is one of three golf courses in Thailand designed by the prolific California-based architect, Ronald Fream, who has become something of an Asian specialist (see also pp.58–59). His initial effort in Bangkok, Panya Indra, has a highly decorative 27 holes including 18 that can be totally illuminated for night-time play.

Panya Park is a fine example of turning a problem into a strategic advantage. Potential sites in the Bangkok area tend to be flat and barren, and, with heavy clay soil and poor natural drainage, they are prone to flooding and have few existing trees. Fream's challenge was to create a visually attractive and memorably

scenic golf course, one that could test better players without humiliating the average, yet still be maintainable in conditions of heat, humidity and heavy seasonal rain. The result is a series of holes with soft, sweeping lines, and a very natural feel, with the inevitable water kept well below the level of play, strategically affecting all but one of the 27 holes.

The three interchangeable nines – A, B and C – flow out from a large, centrally sited clubhouse. This is a golfing experience to enjoy, with long flowing contours on the undulating fairways and a variety of generous, gently scalloped bunkers, mainly protecting the greens. The putting surfaces themselves, full of movement and interest, are usually elevated, reached over water, sand and the usual trademark of tumbled rocks in front and a ring of palms behind. All three courses are beautifully maintained, with some nice patches of floral decoration and a good selection of quickly maturing trees.

Two of the most memorable holes turn up on the B course. The par 3 3rd, 167yd/153m, could be classed as the club's signature hole. It is completely flat but played from a richly floral, elevated tee to a deep, elevated green. Its significant feature is that, in between, one is faced with a veritable sea of sand, a series of green hummocks rising from the billowing, swirling expanse of bunker that stretches from

PANYA PARK A				PANYA PARK B				PANYA PARK C			
HOLE	YD	M	PAR	HOLE	YD	M	PAR	HOLE	YD	M	PAR
1	418	382	4	1	436	399	4	1	403	368	4
2	390	357	4	2	416	380	4	2	359	328	4
3	377	345	4	3	167	153	3	3	201	184	3
4	514	470	5	4	531	485	5	4	414	378	4
5	218	199	3	5	189	173	3	5	566	517	5
6	548	501	5	6	402	367	4	6	467	427	4
7	168	154	3	7	532	486	5	7	367	336	4
8	388	355	4	8	371	339	4	8	196	179	3
9	410	375	4	9	429	392	4	9	524	479	5
TOTAL	3431	3137	36	TOTAL	3473	3175	36	TOTAL	3497	3198	36
3431YD • 3137M • PAR 36				3473YD • 3175M • PAR 36				3497YD • 3198M • PAR 36			

the tee all the way up to and around the green. Apart from the psychological effect, judgement of distance is deceptive. Another memorable hole is the 8th, a medium-length 371yd/339m par 4. Alternate fairways beckon across a lake – that on the left offering a relatively safe dogleg route into the green across sand; the other seductively requiring a heroic carry over water on a direct route between palms and several bunkers to seriously shorten the approach. Plenty of sand and water, with very little of the short stuff, make this a real chancer's challenge.

The monumental clubhouse, with its tall glazed galleries and palatial carpeted staircases, seems strangely out of place in such a natural golfing environment. But the locker rooms are functional, the pro-shop adequate and from the spacious Chuan Chom restaurant upstairs, you can choose from a varied menu while enjoying

Above: Golfer and caddies reach the water-ringed green of the par 4 3rd A course.

sweeping views out over the course. Add in a small army of helpful, friendly caddies waiting by the clubhouse entrance as you arrive and your day is complete, whatever your score.

The course designer, Ronald Fream, is well aware of the overriding need to build golf courses that can remain playable in all tropical weathers. Equally, he combines an artistic flair with pragmatism to create golf to delight as well as test players at all levels.

Below: A sea of sand and rolling mounds protects the shot to the par 3 3rd B course.

11 *President Country Club*

*President Country Club, 42 Moo 8, Suwintawongse
Road, Lumtoiting, Nonjok, Bangkok 10530*
TEL: *(02) 988 7555-63* **FAX:** *(02) 988 7564*
EMAIL: *president@bkk.loxinfo.co.th*
LOCATION: *15km east of Minburi; Route 304*
COURSE: *36 holes: North 3555yd/3250m;
East 3416yd/3123m; West 3533yd/3230m;
South 3559yd/3254m; all par 36*
TYPE OF COURSE: *Level parkland with considerable
strategic water*
DESIGNER: *Robert Trent Jones Jr (1994)*
GREEN FEES: *BB*
FACILITIES: *Golf shop, caddies, cart and golf equipment
hire, shoe, umbrella and chair rental, driving range,
bunker, chipping and putting greens, changing facilities,
sauna, Jacuzzi, refreshment shelters on course, restaurant
in clubhouse*
VISITORS: *Welcome, but advance reservation necessary*

PRESIDENT COUNTRY CLUB

NORTH COURSE	YD	M	PAR	EAST COURSE	YD	M	PAR
1	505	462	5	10	349	319	4
2	401	367	4	11	518	474	5
3	209	191	3	12	431	394	4
4	415	379	4	13	333	304	4
5	429	392	4	14	154	141	3
6	177	162	3	15	405	370	4
7	383	350	4	16	588	538	5
8	469	429	4	17	197	180	3
9	567	518	5	18	441	403	4
	3555	3250	36	IN	3416	3123	36

6971YD • 6373M • PAR 72

M any golf clubs around Bangkok were
built in the early 1990s, when
investment was plentiful, and dreams of real
estate fortunes clouded realism. This often
shifted priorities from golf to other facilities,
resulting in vast clubhouses of glass and
marble that were more like palaces – majestic
entrances and approach avenues – with the
golf playing second fiddle.

Fortunately, President Country Club,
although conceived in this era, has never
wavered from the need to provide a first-class
golf club for its members, their guests and
visitors. Its courses are of international class,

and have already hosted a number of
important events. In asking Robert Trent
Jones Jr to create 36 holes over what was rice
paddy just north-east of the city, the club
made an inspired choice.

Trent Jones has done an excellent job,
combining playable golf from the members'
tees with serious challenges from the back.
On what was essentially flat, uninspiring land,
he has created four nine-hole loops, each of
slightly different character, all with the
undulating flow of a genuine golfing
challenge, and all with a quaintly 'Scottish'
feel. This is particularly noticeable in the open
foregreen areas, which leave opportunities for
a running long iron approach or pitch and
run, a shot rarely playable on most Bermuda
grass layouts. There is also the novelty of the
vast double green fronting the clubhouse,
which serves the final holes of both South and
East courses, with the possibility (shades of St
Andrews) of a 160-ft/48-m putt!

The undulations and mounding are gentle,
and highly reminiscent of the Scottish
tradition, as is the prevailing breeze, which
changes direction with the seasons. An
excellently designed drainage system ensures
play under all conditions. Strategic placement
is required to avoid scalloped areas of sand
and large lakes, while the firm, fast greens
have many subtle slopes. Away from play,

PRESIDENT COUNTRY CLUB

WEST COURSE	YD	M	PAR	SOUTH COURSE	YD	M	PAR
1	514	470	5	10	413	378	4
2	440	402	4	11	557	509	5
3	165	151	3	12	189	173	3
4	384	351	4	13	439	401	4
5	405	370	4	14	432	395	4
6	437	400	4	15	347	317	4
7	556	508	5	16	461	421	4
8	185	169	3	17	159	145	3
9	447	409	4	18	562	514	5
IN	3533	3230	36	OUT	3559	3254	36

7092YD • 6434M • PAR 72

Above: A tough shot on the par 3 17th East course over water and sand to an elevated, angled green.
Below: The imposing Spanish-style clubhouse.

native grasslands and lagoons form a sanctuary for birds and other wildlife.

The West/South combination is the tougher test of the two 18s. At nearly 7100yd/6492m off the gold tees, it presents a fair if demanding challenge. A number of long par 4s will tempt the big hitter, but these are offset by medium-length short holes. The last two holes on the South make a fine finish. The 17th is a 159-yd/145-m par 3, played across water to an angled, sloping green protected by three bunkers behind.

The last hole is a real monster at 562yd/514m off the tips, with a thirsty lake all along the right-hand side and across the front of the well-bunkered multi-tier green shared with the East course. In contrast, the North/East course plays a little shorter, with a number of sharp, tempting doglegs to encourage the bold.

The impressive, Spanish-style clubhouse offers excellent amenities. Two restaurants with panoramic golf course views offer Thai, Chinese, Japanese and international menus plus dim sum at lunchtime. There is also a well-stocked pro-shop plus a sports club, with pool, fitness club and massage.

12 *Thai Country Club*

Thai Country Club, 88 Moo 1, Bangna–Trad Road Km 35.5, Thambon Pimpa, Bangpakong District, Chachoengsao 24180
TEL: *(038) 570 234-46* **FAX:** *(038) 570 225*
EMAIL: *thaiclub@loxinfo.co.th*
LOCATION: *Off Route 34 at Km 35.5*
COURSE: *18 holes, 7052yd/6248m, par 72*
TYPE OF COURSE: *Well-landscaped championship course with much strategic sand and water*
DESIGNER: *Dennis Griffiths (1996)*
GREEN FEES: *BBBBB*
FACILITIES: *Golf shop, caddies, cart and golf equipment hire, shoe and umbrella rental, driving range, putting green, changing facilities, spa with sauna and massage, five refreshment shelters on course, bar and restaurant in clubhouse*
VISITORS: *Private members club. Guests of Peninsula Hotel, Bangkok welcome; other visitors should apply in advance by letter*

HOLE	YD	M	PAR	HOLE	YD	M	PAR
1	375	343	4	10	406	371	4
2	362	331	4	11	161	147	3
3	205	187	3	12	449	411	4
4	502	459	5	13	415	379	4
5	424	388	4	14	600	549	5
6	218	199	3	15	423	387	4
7	507	464	5	16	179	164	3
8	410	375	4	17	570	521	5
9	414	378	4	18	432	396	4
OUT	3417	3124	36	IN	3417	3124	36

THAI COUNTRY CLUB

7052YD • 6248M • PAR 72

It is probably true that most readers will never have the particular pleasure of playing here. But in recommending the best golf in Thailand, it would be a grave omission not to include what is a very special and equally extremely private members' club. Thai Country Club is certainly the most expensive but also the best-maintained and serviced course in the country. Less than an hour down the highway south-west of Bangkok, on the site of an original golf course from the early 1980s, this is a supreme example of what can be achieved with the right budget, expertise and commitment to excellence by all concerned. It unashamedly sets out to offer its members the ultimate in luxury, a quality experience from the moment they enter the property, without ever losing sight of the fact that this is first and foremost a golf club. It bears out Walter Hagen's dictum that he might not have been a millionaire but he intended to live like one.

The 18-hole course, designed by Dennis Griffiths, is every golfer's dream. Gently undulating and mounded, it flows past flowering trees and shrubs, with a sea breeze off the Gulf of Siam whispering through the palm trees.

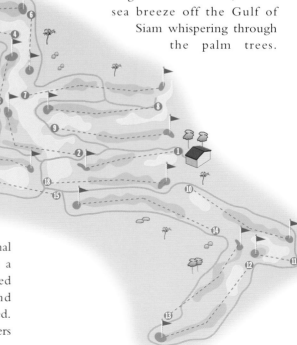

Manicured beyond belief, you can be sure of a perfect lie on the paspalum grass fairways, and the rough is reasonable. This is a course that the members can enjoy, while it can still test the Tiger. There is a touch of Florida, a touch of magic, golf in heaven – even the palms are replete with coconuts. All the hazards are visible, from splashes of scalloped white sand to attractive lakes. No expense has been spared, either on the course or off, to achieve the ultimate golfing experience.

Two major events have been played here to date. The Asian Honda Classic, in 1997, saw Tiger Woods win with 20 under par, including driving the 10th green (372yd/340m from the blue tee). In 1998, Vijay Singh took the second leg of the Johnnie Walker Super Tour here, while his partner Ernie Els rated it 'in the best condition of any course I've played in Asia'.

The club is managed by the Peninsula Hotel group, in joint venture with Thai ownership, and their experience of providing a luxurious lifestyle is apparent throughout. The facilities and service will stand comparison anywhere in

Above: A true challenge at the par 3 6th hole.
Below: The lakeside clubhouse overlooks the 18th green.

the world, whether in the elegant, panoramic restaurant, the members' bar or the superb spa locker rooms with sauna, steam rooms, hot pool, massage and individual marble jet therapy showers. The course refreshment stops are open-air restaurants; the pro-shop is comprehensive and the caddies immaculate.

13 Subhapruek

Subhapruek Golf Course, 102 Moo 7, Bangna–Trad Road Km 26, Bangbor, Samutprakarn 10560
TEL: *(02) 317 0801-4, 316 2636* **FAX:** *(02) 317 0805*
LOCATION: *At Km 26 on Route 34*
COURSE: *18 holes, 7010yd/6410m, par 72*
TYPE OF COURSE: *Gently flowing tropical parkland on a level site*
DESIGNER: *Dye Design Inc (1993)*
GREEN FEES: *BB*
FACILITIES: *Golf shop, caddies, equipment hire, shoe, chair and umbrella rental, driving range, putting green, changing facilities, refreshment shelters on course, restaurant in clubhouse*
VISITORS: *Welcome, but advance reservation advised*

Well established and very popular (with as many as 300 players on a public holiday), this club does what it does very well, while at the same time failing to conform with the majority. It is one of the few courses in Thailand that does not have a fleet of rental golf carts – so walking is required. Another unusual feature is that it has 19 holes – the last a fully fledged par 3 played from elevated tees over water, which can be alternated into the main course as required – or used to settle tied matches! The monolithic clubhouse, which resembles an ancient stone temple, leads you into facilities all comfortably sited at ground level. The restaurant has an international menu including Thai, Chinese and Japanese (with the sashimi flown fresh from Japan), wine and an excellent ambience. Its terrace looks out over a formal flower garden and waterfall to the elevated 10th tee.

Large, scalloped bunkers, some greens shored up by railway sleepers (a Dye Design Inc trademark), mature palms, much water and colourful flowering trees are features of this gently undulating course, as are the host of well-trained female caddies in crushed raspberry outfits. The 16th, 150yd/137m from the elevated tee, is a memorable par 3, all carry across water to a small green surrounded by a necklace of large, intimidating rocks.

Below: Much water and ranks of mature palm trees are key strategic features on this course.

14 Bangpakong Riverside

Bangpakong Riverside Country Club, 49 Moo 2, Bangkok–Chachoengsao Road, Sanpudart, Banpoh, Chachoengsao 24140
TEL: *(038) 513 523-5* **FAX:** *(038) 513 526*
LOCATION: *Route 314 off Route 34 at Km 47*
COURSE: *18 holes, 7140yd/6529m, par 72*
TYPE OF COURSE: *Level exposed riverside parkland course with many additional water hazards*
DESIGNER: *Chird Boonyaratanavej (1990)*
GREEN FEES: *BB*
FACILITIES: *Golf shop, caddies, cart and golf equipment hire, shoe rental, driving range, putting green, changing facilities, sauna, refreshment shelters on course, restaurants in clubhouse. Member facilities include tennis courts, swimming pool, watersports centre, fitness room, snooker and games*
VISITORS: *Welcome, but advance telephone call advised*

This course is set alongside the banks of the Bangpakong River with its natural wildlife habitat, about halfway on the route from Bangkok to Pattaya just before Chonburi. The club offers everything on a grand scale. From the massive clubhouse, with its large balcony and air-conditioned restaurants overlooking the course, to the two-tiered driving range and sports complex and the huge practice putting greens, the course has been designed on a broad canvas.

The golf course itself, long by any standards at 7140yd/6529m off the back, has wide, friendly fairways, but plays its full length, with little run on the ball. On a very level landscape, with spacious, shallow bunkers, this is comfortable golf, with little fairway movement, where big hitters will be in their element. The well-established trees pose little hazard, everything is very lush and green, with an army of ground staff keeping everything in beautiful condition. There are no easy holes, despite the open nature of the course – they all tend to play long. However, you get good lies on the fairways, there are colourful splashes of floral colour and a friendly welcome. The course is not too busy midweek, with an excellent-value green fee.

Below: The extensive and well-appointed clubhouse towers over the sloping final green.

History of Golf

The current explosion of holiday golf worldwide has underlined Thailand's place as a highly attractive destination. But few realize that the game has been played there for more than a century. As in many other far-flung places, where the British (and particularly Scottish) went or had influence, golf soon followed.

It has been said that when two or three British people get together, they inevitably form a club. Colonial links with India and Myanmar saw British trading companies, particularly in timber, established in the northern Siamese city of Chiang Mai. In 1898, 14 of these expatriates met to form the 'Chiengmai Gymkhana Club', to encourage all kinds of sport, and to buy appropriate land. Among them were Louis Leonowens, whose mother Anna was immortalized on film for her time as teacher in the royal household (*The King and I*), and W.W. Wood, whose son Dick remains a life patron of the club today.

Above: More than a century old, the giant rain tree is part of Chiangmai Gymkhana Club history

A key feature of the club was a horse-racing circuit, which in turn provided opportunities at the 1899 Christmas Meeting for 'two days races, a polo tournament, cricket, athletic sports, tennis and golf, for a challenge silver niblick presented by Mr Parratt'. Sepia photographs in the bar plus the club minutes show that the nine holes of golf prospered, including local rules to cover the grazing rights of bullocks and buffalos. Thais were first considered for membership in 1941. Today, with more than 300 members, predominantly Thai, the Gymkhana Club offers a fascinating link with the past. Its golf course and clubhouse are dominated by a massive rain tree (older than the club itself), and the place is steeped in history and ageless charm.

Just as the British tended to export their sporting culture wherever they went, so interest in European ways and fashion attracted the Thai royal family and Bangkok's elite at the turn of the century. Land for a horse-racing circuit was granted by King Rama V in 1901, to become the Royal Bangkok Sports Club. This is now an exclusive multi-sports club with 18 holes of golf within and across the race track, a green oasis in the centre of the city's downtown high-rises. Soon after, in 1903, the first nine holes of the Royal Turf Club (now Dusit) were also created within another horse-racing oval. With a further central Bangkok course (now no longer in existence) within the Chitralada Palace itself, these formed the extent of golf for interested royalty and well-connected foreigners for the next 20 years.

After visits to Europe, the King came to appreciate the perceived medical advantages of seaside recuperation and bathing. He purchased a steamer so that his family could escape the torrid heat and humidity of the capital for the cooling breezes of the Gulf of Siam. However, it was the extension of the railway south-west to Malaysia that led to the establishment of a palace, fashionable holiday homes and a hotel

at Hua Hin, with a nine-hole golf course right by the railway station, in 1924 (see p.132). The royal family were ardent players, shown in a contemporary photograph in striped blazers, plus fours and topees, hickory shafts at the ready. The course was extended to 18 holes in 1925. It was the first purpose-built resort golf course in Thailand, catering to visitors to the original Railway Hotel, which 'maintains a stock of golf requisites … and possesses one of

the best golf courses in the Orient' (*Guide to Bangkok*, 1926).

A preserve of a privileged few, golf expanded no further until the 1950s, when government agencies, including the Army, Navy and Air Force, started to create further sporting facilities of their own. The unique 'runway' course at Don Muang (see p.90) appeared in 1956, and the Tourist Office built an 18-hole golf resort at Bangpra in 1958. The first private enterprise resort courses, Siam Country Club and The Rose Garden, opened in 1972, followed the next year by the World Cup venue of Navatanee.

The 1990s saw the game expand rapidly with the appearance of many modern clubs and courses. Despite recent economic problems, there are now 182 courses in play.

Above: Bangkok's 18-hole Dusit course still runs inside and around the horse-race track.
Below: Royal Hua Hin's 1st tee, ancient locomotive and elegant Royal waiting room on the station platform

REGIONAL DIRECTORY

Where to Stay

Bangkok

The Dusit Thani (02 236 0450-9, Fax: 02 236 6400) Now in its 31st year, this flagship hotel of the Dusit group maintains the highest international standards with a distinctly Thai flavour. Set in the heart of Bangkok's main business and entertainment district, it has resisted the trend created by bland, faceless 'global' hotels. It preserves the essentially Thai quality of its welcome, personalized service and luxury facilities that have proved so appealing over the years. The 530 guest rooms, including Landmark and other opulent suites with private butler service, have décor that reflects the craftsmanship and culture of the country's past. Fine dining includes Royal Thai cuisine in the Benjarong, exquisite Chinese in the Mayflower or less formal offerings in Chinatown. Alternative Asian tastes are met in the Thien Duong Vietnamese restaurant or the authentic Japanese Shogun. Western dishes, including prime beef, feature at Hamilton's and the rooftop Tiara, while the Pavilion offers all-day choice including an excellent lunchtime buffet with succulent fresh seafood. For the more active, there is a pool, fitness centre, a new spa and a roof-top golf driving range.

The Oriental (02 236 0400, Fax: 02 236 1937) Celebrating its 125th anniversary in 2001, this historic hotel retains its hallmark sense of tradition. With more than 1000 staff committed to ultimate levels of service, it has regularly been voted the world's best hotel. The original hotel building has been retained, but further integrated construction now provides a total of 395 luxuriously appointed rooms and suites on the edge of the Chao Phraya River. All have a river view, and all floors have butler service. No less than ten restaurants and bars provide a selection to suit all tastes. Try the Normandie for classic French; China House for Cantonese; Lord Jim's for seafood and international cuisine; the Verandah coffee shop for a Thai and international menu; the Riverside Terrace for al fresco steak and seafood barbecues; and Ciao for Italian. Rim Naam Thai and its Sala adds classical dance, while the Bamboo bar combines drinks with live jazz. The Author's Lounge, in the original hotel, offers traditional afternoon tea. There is also a spa, beauty salon and barber, two pools, gym, tennis, squash, sauna and steam. Novel features include a Thai cooking and culture school, daily river cruise to Ayutthaya, complete golf arrangements and, for the really well-heeled, a helicopter service from the airport.

The Pan Pacific (02 632 9000, Fax: 02 632 9001) Occupying the top ten floors of a 32-storey tower overlooking the Silom intersection, it is ideally placed for shopping, the night market and its adjacent nightlife and has spectacular views out over the city. In addition to the elegantly furnished guest rooms, the two Pacific Floors offer the ultimate in secluded, personalized service with private butler and numerous complimentary benefits. The large number of Japanese guests speaks volumes for the efficiency of its service and the quality of the Keyaki Japanese restaurant. Alternatively, diners can enjoy Cantonese fare at Hai Tien Lo or the international menu on the 23rd floor Heights Café. There is a fully equipped gymnasium, a swimming pool on the roof and a relaxing sauna and Clinique spa. Golf can be arranged through the Business Centre.

Grand Pacific Hotel (02 651 1000, Fax; 02 255 2441) In the centre of Sukhumvit, this hotel is ideally located for the airport expressway, the Skytrain and the wide range of shopping and nightlife in this popular area. All 388 guest rooms and suites offer skyline views with satellite TV and in-house movies, well-stocked minibar plus tea and coffee, with butler service on the Signature floors. Japanese food is available at Kisso, Cantonese at Ho Kitchen, regional Thai food at Hot Chillies and international fare at The Captain's Table, including a very popular Sunday buffet brunch. There is also a gym, pool, sauna and beauty salon with massage.

Pathumwan Princess (02 216 3700-29, Fax: 02 216 3730-3) This hotel is ideally located for shopping. It is right next to the Mahboonkrong shopping arcade, Siam Square and close to the World Trade Centre. Described as 'state-of-the-art', it is 29 floors high, all immaculately furnished and with a full range of amenities. Thai and international food is served round the clock at the Lobby Bistro, while, for something a bit different, Kongju specializes in Korean cuisine. Facilities include a pool, roof-top tennis court, squash, fitness centre, sauna and steam rooms.

Nakhon Pathom

The Rose Garden Hotel (034 322 588-93, Fax: 034 322 775) Located in a verdant riverside setting a short distance west of Bangkok, this hotel provides an opportunity to unwind, 'smell the flowers' and play a little golf (see p.30). It is also close enough to visit the 'City of Angels' for some shopping or sightseeing. It is a country resort offering peace and relaxation with its light and airy poolside coffee shop or more traditional Japanese restaurant. One feels like a private house guest, because of the original paintings and furnishings and the unobtrusive but attentive service. There is little sign that this is, in fact, a very well-organized 160-room hotel. A short stroll through the gardens leads you to a traditional teak-built Thai restaurant

Above: Traditional Thailand – vegetable carving, rich teak and elegant woven silk.

moored over the river. Every afternoon, a cultural show offers a snapshot glimpse of the many colourful aspects of the country. There is a pool, tennis facilities, snooker, fitness centre and steam rooms. A comprehensive spa will open shortly. The classic golf course remains a short distance away by hotel shuttle.

Where to Eat
Bangkok
Prik Kee Noo (02 631 2324-5) Coffee shop-style Thai food with true chilli flavours; somewhat spicy. **Seafood Palace** (02 653 3900-5) Select your own fresh seafood, fish plus wine and dine in classic splendour. **Café de Paris** (02 237 2776) Small atmospheric bistro with French menu and daily specials in the heart of Patpong. **Le Café Siam** (02 671 0030-1) Colonial house with classic French specialities. **The Barbican** (02 234 3590) Very British pub-restaurant. Popular, with different dining/drinking levels. **Bobby's Arms** (02 233 6828) Small no-frills British pub with roast beef and fish and chips. **Himali Cha Cha** (02 258 8843) True Himalayan Indian cuisine with flair. **Trattoria da Roberto** (02 233 6851) Upstairs Italian restaurant maintaining simple but authentic Italian menu overlooking busy Patpong II. **Kongju** (02 216 3700) In Pathumwan Princess Hotel, close to MBK shops, very popular Korean restaurant with individual charcoal barbecues and healthy choice. **Koreana** (02 252 9398) Large and busy with many authentic Korean specialities. **Le Dalat Indochine** (02 661 7967-8) Classic Vietnamese cuisine served in elegant ethnic surroundings. **Lyon** (02 253 8141) Not cheap, but traditional French cooking and wine served with style. **Benjarong** (02 236 0450) Truly regal surroundings in the Dusit Thani hotel to enjoy Royal Thai cuisine. A memorable, upmarket dining experience. **Baan Suan** (02 261 6650) Affordable Thai food in an authentic atmosphere at Sukhumvit. **Paesano** (02 252 2834) Noted Italian restaurant; offers a hotel pickup service in a London taxi.

What to See
Ancient Bangkok edges the winding Chao Phraya River. (For details on the main royal palaces, temples and other places of interest, see pp.24-25.) Outside Bangkok, visit the traditional floating market at Damnoen Saduak, the nearby temple and *chedi* at Nakhon Pathom and the cultural show at The Rose Garden. About an hour north of the city lies the ruined city of Ayutthaya. This was founded in 1350 and was the capital of Siam for more than 400 years. Close by is the beautiful Royal Summer Palace at Bang Pa-In (see back cover).

Chapter 2

Eastern
Seaboard

In this beautiful country that attracts tourists from around the world, it is somewhat perverse that the region with the most (and several of the best) holiday golf courses has the least to offer in terms of natural and historic sights, ethnic groups or local crafts. The east coast, which runs down from the mouth of Bangkok's Chao Phraya river some 500km (310 miles) to the border with Cambodia, is probably Thailand's best-known and most popular beach resort area. Its main seaside city, Pattaya, is less than a two-hour drive south-east from Bangkok. In its very rapid and uncontrolled development, the area has become something of a victim of its own

success, endeavouring to be all things to all people in a brash and breezy man-made holiday environment. Traditional

Left: A tranquil beach with tall coconut palms on Ko Samet, Rayong. Above: 'Khlong boys' find an errant golf ball in a flower-rimmed water hazard.

Thailand this is not, but as an international playground for sun worshippers, watersports fanatics, bargain shoppers, food lovers and nightbirds of all persuasions, it is unrivalled.

Some 40 years ago, this was a comparatively somnolent coastline of small fishing villages. American troops, recuperating from the pressures of the Vietnam War, discovered Pattaya, whose only previous claim to fame had been as an overnight resting place for the army of the Thai King Narai in the 13th century. The continuing interest of the Americans and considerable local efforts to provide suitable facilities led to the growth of what is now a highly colourful, sprawling clash of cultures, and the country's main beach resort. Improving road communications encouraged residents of Bangkok to use their cars and spend weekends there and along other parts of the coastline. This created an emergent holiday infrastructure.

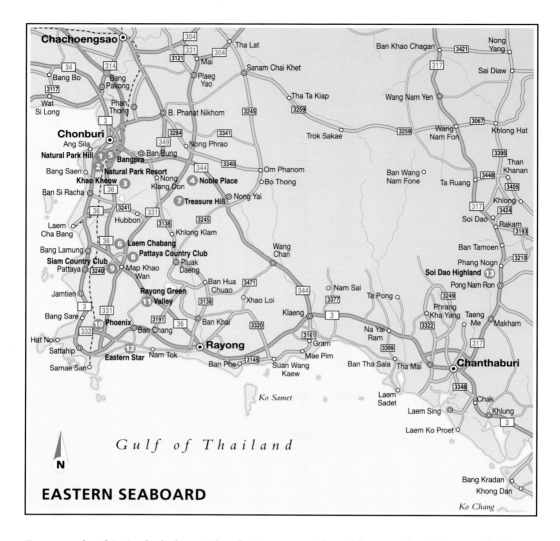

EASTERN SEABOARD

Fortunately, this included a wide choice of vacation golf courses, many including second homes and condominiums as part of their development.

The east coast also offers a succession of contrasts. Downtown Pattaya offers 24-hour hedonism, but there are also some top-class hotels, secluded in out-of-town seaside locations, and a truly international choice of restaurants, many serving fresh-caught fish and seafood. Golfers are spoiled for choice, with no less than 20 courses, several with 27 holes, within

comfortable reach. Many of these, designed by world-famous names, provide excellent tests of the game in scenic settings. Perhaps the finest example is the course at Soi Dao Highland. Situated a little further east near the Cambodian border, it is one of the most dramatic and beautiful in the country.

Further down the coast towards Rayong are long stretches of less busy beaches. Here visitors have the prospect of spending time on one of several nearby islands, either in the Ko Lan group, popular Ko

Samet or the uncluttered palm-fringed paradise of Ko Chang near Trat, Thailand's second largest island, with its white sands, clear water and simple beach bungalow accommodation. Visitors on their way to play golf beneath the majestic mountain of Khao Soi Dao will pass through Chanthaburi, a town famous for trade in gem stones, as the home of Thailand's largest Christian cathedral (built in the early 18th century) and as a regional centre

Above: The warm waters of the Gulf of Thailand and superb beaches are popular with tourists.

for three exotic fruits – durian, rambutan and mangosteen, which prompt their own local festival in June. At the other end of the coast, just after the provincial capital of Chonburi, is the tiny unspoiled fishing village of Ang Sila. Here visitors will find superb seafood and fine samples of the local handicraft, stone pestles and mortars.

THAI BOXING

A version of Thai boxing is promoted to tourists, as is the case with bullfighting in Spain. However, the true sport of Muay Thai or kick boxing, developed from an ancient martial art, has a following of keen fans who support and bet on their favourites vociferously. Matches are often held three times weekly at such venues as the Lumphini Stadium ring in Bangkok. Thai boxing is Thailand's most popular spectator sport (unless you count those night owls who sit glued to television programmes showing European football matches). After much introductory ceremony and paying homage to their teachers, two professional opponents, wearing boxing gloves but no footwear, attack each other ferociously with their feet, knees, elbows and fists. In fact, any part of the body can be used except the head. The fighting is carried out to the wailing accompaniment of a three-instrument band.

Natural Park Hill

Natural Park Hill Golf Club, 159/1 Moo 2,
Saensuk–Bangpra Road, Muang, Chonburi 20130
TEL: *(038) 393 001-18* **FAX:** *(038) 393 019*
LOCATION: *Route 3144 via Route 3 at Km 83*
marker
COURSE: *18 holes, 6807yd/6224m, par 72*
TYPE OF COURSE: *Well-contoured championship*
layout on sloping land with variety of mature trees
DESIGNER: *Ronald Fream (1992)*
GREEN FEES: *BB*
FACILITIES: *Golf shop, caddies, cart and golf equipment*
hire, umbrella and shoe rental, driving range, putting
green, changing facilities, refreshment shelters on course,
restaurant in clubhouse
VISITORS: *Advance booking necessary*

NATURAL PARK HILL

HOLE	YD	M	PAR	HOLE	YD	M	PAR
1	409	374	4	10	370	338	4
2	392	358	4	11	535	489	5
3	555	507	5	12	376	344	4
4	381	348	4	13	402	368	4
5	152	139	3	14	582	532	5
6	558	510	5	15	150	137	3
7	410	375	4	16	325	297	4
8	195	178	3	17	200	183	3
9	398	364	4	18	417	381	4
OUT	3450	3155	36	IN	3357	3070	36

6807YD • 6224M • PAR 72

This course is a treat to the eye, spilling gently downhill below the slopes of a tree-encrusted mountain range with views to the sea. It could also be the toughest resort course in Thailand. Californian designer Ronald Fream welcomed the varied nature of the site – a hillside blessed with 50-year-old mango orchards running down to level land, where water

plus palmyra and silk oak. Then there are the large, highly strategic lakes, which dominate the lower levels. Thirdly, there is the continuous rise and fall of the flowing fairways, a succession of mounds, swales, humps and hollows, which give something of a links character to this essentially parkland layout.

The fairways seem generous from the tee, but careful placement is needed to avoid strategic trees and to find the ideal line to the

would become the prime feature. He relished the challenge and came up with a masterpiece, arguably the finest course he has created in Asia.

There are three main features of the course, which make a major contribution to its difficulty. Firstly there are the trees – giant mangos, tall groves of coconut palm

greens. These are mostly elevated and well protected by deep, mounded areas of sand, which are often below the subtle putting surfaces. It pays to follow your caddie's advice on the putting line; it is often not what it appears. The

hazards are demanding but fair; best advice is not to take on more risk than you can handle.

One of the most challenging holes is undoubtedly the 14th, a left-curving par 5 of 582yd/532m around a large lake. This is all about risk and reward. The fairway tilts towards the water as it curves through at least 90° and is not as narrow as it appears. Unless you get well up with your second, the approach is fraught with danger, needing to carry water, rocks and deep areas of mounded sand to an elevated green with several slopes. For most, bogey is a good score.

Two other holes pose interesting possibilities. The 11th, also a par 5, offers alternate fairways around a wooded copse, the narrower line left yielding the easier approach. The 17th, a very memorable par 3 played across a rock-strewn lake ringed with bougainvillea, has a completely alternate tee and green, played along the left side of the water.

The large clubhouse has panoramic views over the course. It has a pleasant coffee shop and is refreshingly unpretentious.

Above: The hazardous approach to the par 5 3rd, where water, rocks and sand guard the elevated green.

Below: Bougainvillea frames the tougher challenge of the two alternate 17th holes.

2 *Natural Park Resort*

Natural Park Resort Golf Club, 502 Moo 10,
Bangpra, Sriracha, Chonburi 20210
TEL: *(038) 349 370-81* **FAX:** *(038) 349 365;*
349 383
LOCATION: *At Km 83.5 on Route 3 south-east of*
Bangkok
COURSE: *27 holes: A 3526yd/3224m; B*
3483yd/3185m; C 3480yd/3182m; all par 36
TYPE OF COURSE: *Relatively level course with many*
mature palms, strategic bunkers and water
DESIGNER: *Thai Takenaka (1988)*
GREEN FEES: *BB*
FACILITIES: *Golf shop, caddies, cart and golf equipment*
hire, shoe and umbrella rental, driving range, putting
green, changing facilities, sauna, fitness centre with gym,
sports complex with tennis, swimming pool, badminton
and snooker, refreshment shelters on course, restaurant in
clubhouse
VISITORS: *Welcome, but advance booking necessary*

Under the same management as Natural Park Hill, but with golf of a totally different calibre, this is a 27-hole Japanese design of slightly older vintage. It occupies a reasonably level site, with three relatively undemanding loops defined, in the main, by ranks of mature coconut palms. Surprisingly, considering its location, water comes into play on less than half the holes. There is little movement in the broad fairways, and the main problem is one of club judgement to many highly elevated greens, which are often pleasantly shaped and mounded.

The courses are well maintained and any lack of design flair is compensated by areas of colourful on-course floral shrubs, extensive topiary and assembled rocks. This is decorative golf that is well within the range of medium- to high-handicap players.

Away from the golf courses, there is a wide range of other sports and exercise facilities, including a very attractive swimming pool that features its own waterfall. There is also good local and international food available in the coffee shop. The course is overlooked by three huge high-rise condominium towers. Although hardly improving the golfing backdrop, these provide one- and two-bedroom accommodation on-site, with long distance views, at reasonable rates.

Below: Water plays a key role in all six of the short holes on this 27-hole course. From the floral tee of the 7th C, it is all carry to the green.

③ Khao Kheow

Khao Kheow Country Club, 220 Moo 12, Bangpra, Sriracha, Chonburi 20210
TEL: *(038) 298 224-6* **FAX:** *(02) 298 226*
LOCATION: *Approximately 7km east of Bangpra Reservoir. Route 3144 via Route 3*
COURSE: *27 holes: A 3493yd/3194m;*
B 3584yd/3277m; C 3472yd/3175m; all par 36
TYPE OF COURSE: *A valley course with dramatic landscaping and hazards in an open location*
DESIGNER: *Dye Design Inc (1992)*
GREEN FEES: *BB*
FACILITIES: *Golf shop, caddies, cart and golf equipment hire, shoe and umbrella rental, driving range, putting green, changing facilities, refreshment shelters on course, restaurant in new clubhouse*
VISITORS: *Welcome, but advance booking advised; dress code, soft spikes*

Khao Kheow lies part-way between Bangkok and Pattaya. The improved motorway has made it more accessible from town and the imposing split-level clubhouse, opened in 1998, has improved the facilities.

This course is at last maturing into the sort of tropical parkland test it was designed for after many years in the comparative golfing

Above: Typical Dye Design Inc mounds and a lake guard the final green on the B nine. The modern three-storey clubhouse lies below a wooded hill.

wilderness. Set below a large, conical, heavily wooded hill, the clubhouse acts as a focal point for the three nine-hole loops, which radiate in different directions.

Laid out over slopes gently descending from the mountain foothills, the holes move from forested hills to windswept desert punctuated by tall palms. All bear the Dye Design Inc trademarks – level, often narrow, fairways flanked by high, conical mounds, chisel-edged greens with sheer slopes to flat-floored bunkers well below the level, double-tiered fairways, and a 17th hole (the 8th on the B course) with a circular island green surrounded by water. There is a 20-yd/18-m collar of rough and a bunker at the front of this island, before you reach the putting surface, making it a tight target. Expect a fair amount of movement on the often small greens. This is aesthetically unnatural golf in an attractive location.

4 Noble Place

Noble Place Golf Resort & Country Club, 88/8 Moo 6, Klongkiew, Bangbung, Chonburi 20220
Tel: *(01) 982 0382, (01) 484 9069* **Fax:** *(01) 940 3250*
Location: *At Km 71 on Route 331*
Course: *27 holes: A 3500yd/3200m; B 3315yd/3031m; C 3565yd/3260m; all par 36*
Type of course: *Rolling open heathland with links character*
Designers: *Peter W. Thomson and Michael Wolveridge (1994)*
Green fees: *B*
Facilities: *Golf shop, caddies, cart and equipment hire, shoe and umbrella rental, driving range, putting green, changing facilities, refreshment shelters on course, restaurant in clubhouse*
Visitors: *Welcome, but advance reservation suggested. Soft spikes only*

GOLFING THAI STYLE

Apart from the novelty of female caddies, there are other aspects of Thai golf that may surprise you. The six-ball, sometimes known as 'the Thai crocodile', is common. It means players leaving the green as soon as they hole out, teeing off at the next while others are still putting, and caddies keeping the score. Expect also lots of chatter, movement and mobile phones – reverential silence while you play is unusual. Players use official 'drop areas' after going into water, observe 'call' holes at par 3s (allowing the group following to tee-off) and usually gamble, which creates slow play. It is all *sanuk* – having fun.

In the increasingly global world of golf architecture, there are essentially two schools of thought. One is to make a creative statement, to remove and remodel what is there to build a basically artificial landscape in a trademark style. This often involves a demanding test of the golf game over terrain that bears little resemblance to the original. Proponents of this form of golf course design include Jack Nicklaus, Pete and Perry Dye and Desmond Muirhead. The other approach is to create a golf course that is as close to the original form of the land as possible, to set up the strategic golfing examination in ways that

make it seem that the course was always there, long before the hand of man interfered. This approach to golf course design, the natural look, is exemplified in the work of Robert Trent Jones (both father and son), Ronald Fream, Dennis Griffiths, Robin Nelson and, in the case of Noble Place, by the professional partnership of Australians Peter W. Thomson and Michael Wolveridge.

Peter W. Thomson won the British Open championship five times over seaside links courses in England and Scotland. An affection for these ancient bastions of the game is evident in his course architecture, which in

NOBLE PLACE A					NOBLE PLACE B					NOBLE PLACE C			
HOLE	YD	M	PAR		HOLE	YD	M	PAR		HOLE	YD	M	PAR
1	416	380	4		1	343	314	4		1	436	399	4
2	221	202	3		2	181	165	3		2	390	357	4
3	412	377	4		3	413	378	4		3	215	197	3
4	567	518	5		4	550	503	5		4	554	507	5
5	329	301	4		5	177	162	3		5	378	346	4
6	186	170	3		6	369	337	4		6	167	153	3
7	545	498	5		7	402	368	4		7	562	514	5
8	378	346	4		8	497	454	5		8	436	399	4
9	446	408	4		9	383	350	4		9	427	390	4
TOTAL	3500	3200	36		TOTAL	3315	3031	36		TOTAL	3565	3260	36

3500YD • 3200M • PAR 36   3315YD • 3031M • PAR 36   3565YD • 3260M • PAR 36

Thailand includes Royal Chiangmai, Rayong Green Valley and Noble Place. The latter's 27 holes flow over an exposed, undulating rural landscape formerly devoted to pineapple and tapioca cultivation – tropical heathland open to refreshing breezes off the Gulf of Thailand. The holes feature gentle mounding, clumps of native grasses, pot bunkers, sloping lies, visual foreshortening, grassy swales, humps and hollows, open approaches to excellent greens – all the features of an inland links, backed by a scattering of tropical palm trees and distant views of mountains.

The overriding impression is of a very natural, unspoiled location – a perfect place to relax and unwind. New management is currently improving the level of course maintenance over land that has the potential for more golf in the future. Located between Bangkok and Pattaya, this is another example of a real-estate-based project on hold with excellent golf in play at bargain prices.

The most memorable holes come at the end of each nine,

Above: Rising to the clubhouse, the 9th fairway B.
Below: Natural golf in a rolling heathland setting.

rising uphill to the clubhouse. The 9th on the A course has a shoulder in the fairway, which must be reached to avoid an uphill lie. It is slightly dogleg left, with water and trees left and a nest of three 'Scottish' bunkers on the corner, mounding along the right. It also has a large sand dune containing two bunkers, 40yd/37m short and hiding the small green. The 9th on the B is a classic hole (see p.20). On the C course, the 9th is all risk and reward across a lake, with a cluster of sand beyond.

5 Bangpra

Bangpra International Golf Club, 45 Moo 6, Tambon
Bangpra, Amphur Sriracha, Chonburi 20210
TEL: *(038) 341 149-150* **FAX:** *(038) 341 151*
EMAIL: *bangpra@ptty2.loxinfo.co.th*
LOCATION: *Off Route 3 at Km 110, approx 80*
minutes from Bangkok
COURSE: *18 holes, 7189yd/6574m, par 72*
TYPE OF COURSE: *Long-established testing parkland*
course in wooded mountain valley; reconstructed in 1987
DESIGNER: *TAT and Japan Golf Promotion Co. Ltd.*
(1958, 1987)
GREEN FEES: *BB*
FACILITIES: *Golf shop, caddies, cart and golf equipment*
hire, shoe and umbrella rental, driving range, putting
green, changing facilities, on-site hotel with tennis and
swimming pool, refreshment shelters on course, restaurant
in clubhouse
VISITORS: *Welcome; best to telephone in advance*

This was the first of the 'modern' post-war golf courses, created with enthusiasm by the then Tourist Association of Thailand. Still an excellent golfing challenge, it sits in a gently sloping valley, sheltered by massive wooded hills not far from the sea.

The majority shareholding was taken by Japan Golf Promotion Co. Ltd., who upgraded and partially redesigned the course in 1987. The result is a most attractive place to play, with good old-fashioned golf laid out among large, mature trees in fine condition. There are tall palms, casurinas and flowering trees in purple and pink, echoing the uniforms of the caddies clad in pink with white caps. The setting is colourful and beautiful, an enclosed world apart and an excellent test of the game.

BANGPRA

HOLE	YD	M	PAR	HOLE	YD	M	PAR
1	433	396	4	10	354	324	4
2	206	188	3	11	575	526	5
3	453	414	4	12	206	188	3
4	460	421	4	13	402	367	4
5	533	487	5	14	405	370	4
6	397	363	4	15	541	495	5
7	622	569	5	16	374	342	4
8	221	202	3	17	228	208	3
9	368	336	4	18	411	376	4
OUT	3693	3377	36	IN	3496	3197	36

7189YD • 6574M • PAR 72

Despite the steep surrounding hills, the fairways are only mildly sloped, the bunkers are relatively shallow and there is little mounding. However, the course is no pushover. The holes play long, mature trees impinge on the playing line, and the greens, especially downhill, are very fast. A novel feature is that the tee markers, respectively black, blue, white and red, are in the shape of small elephants. The general improvement in 1987 included the installation of automatic irrigation and a rebuilding of the front nine to incorporate more water hazards, which now affect two-thirds of the opening holes.

The 1st hole, which avoids water, is one of the best opening holes in the country (see feature p.18).

The 8th (see photo p.8) is a long 221-yd/ 202-m hole played slightly downhill across a lake-filled chasm to a sloping plateau green backed by a tree-covered mountainside. It is a good example of the more modern design introduced to the course. One hole from the original course is the par 4 16th. This is not too long, but is totally dominated by an enormous tree sited centrally in the fairway. There are bunkers left and right, with more crossing the fairway beyond the tree and others around the green. Accuracy here is far more important than length.

The colonial-style clubhouse has Japanese baths and an elegant upstairs restaurant with an extensive menu. Right next door is an equally tasteful 57-room resort hotel with its own garden swimming pool. This is a very

Above: The 17th is a fine par 3 across water to a green encircled by bunkers. Below: View over the 9th green to clubhouse and resort hotel.

popular spot for a weekend break, especially with Japanese visitors, who can feel truly at home. A pioneer as a purpose-built resort golfing location, just as Royal Hua Hin had been in the 1920s, Bangpra has stood the test of time well. More recent renovation, coupled with the wealth of mature trees and delightful setting among wooded hills, makes it a very pleasant place to play. It is well worth a visit.

🏌️ *Laem Chabang*

Laem Chabang International Country Club, 106/8 Moo 4, Beung, Sriracha, Chonburi 20230
TEL: *(038) 372 273* **FAX:** *(038) 372 275*
WWW: *lcic1977@chonburi.ksc.co.th*
LOCATION: *On Route 36 filter left at Km 32 marker; course is a further 7km, near Klang Dong Reservoir*
COURSE: *27 holes, A 3446yd/3151m; B 3419yd/3126m; C 3619yd/3309m, all par 36*
TYPE OF COURSE: *Championship quality holes laid out over varied terrain from mountain slopes to level lakeland*
DESIGNER: *Jack Nicklaus (1993)*
GREEN FEES: *BBB*
FACILITIES: *Golf shop, caddies, cart and golf equipment hire, also shoe and umbrella rental, driving range, pitching and putting greens, changing facilities, on-course accommodation, swimming pool, beauty salon, massage, snooker, refreshment shelters on course, restaurants in clubhouse*
VISITORS: *Welcome, but advance telephone reservation advisable; dress code*

One's first glimpse of this golf resort is unique. Created in a natural amphitheatre of sheltering wooded hills and rocky outcrops, the whole panorama of the 27-hole golf course with its vast clubhouse and golf lodge is laid out before you, rather like an enormous stage set waiting for the performance to begin. The setting is the prime attraction of playing here. Each of the three nine-hole loops occupies a totally different section of the property, and each has its own individual character. The Mountain nine, set back up among the hills, offers spectacular views, heroic carries over chasms and severe changes of elevation. The Lake nine, in contrast, spills downhill and back again past ranks of palm, with, perhaps surprisingly, only three lakes affecting play. Water is far more of a problem on the highly challenging Valley course, which mostly meanders along a highly strategic watercourse below the main club buildings.

This club is one of five in Thailand bearing the design label of master golfer Jack Nicklaus and is probably the most challenging. Despite his inarguable reputation as a player, golf courses bearing Nicklaus' name have proved contentious, admired by many but considered to be almost unplayable by others. Impartial opinion would suggest that a Nicklaus course is essentially manufactured rather than natural, tending to repetitious design features and generally requiring levels of shotmaking beyond the capacity of most amateur golfers. Such features may well appear as advantages to some, particularly better players. Laem Chabang embodies all the characteristics that have created this reputation. While golf demands a number of courses capable of testing the best players in championship events, it is arguable whether holiday resort layouts should come into this category. Play here to test your game, but do not be surprised if you

A: MOUNTAIN NINE			
HOLE	YD	M	PAR
1	339	310	4
2	175	160	3
3	439	401	4
4	528	483	5
5	412	377	4
6	384	351	4
7	212	194	3
8	536	490	5
9	421	385	4
TOTAL	3446	3151	36

3446YD · 3151M · PAR 36

B: LAKE NINE			
HOLE	YD	M	PAR
1	380	347	4
2	518	473	5
3	422	486	4
4	363	332	4
5	212	194	3
6	441	403	4
7	378	346	4
8	184	168	3
9	521	476	5
TOTAL	3419	3126	36

3419YD · 3126M · PAR 36

C: VALLEY NINE			
HOLE	YD	M	PAR
1	438	400	4
2	538	492	5
3	420	384	4
4	454	415	4
5	205	187	3
6	550	503	5
7	419	383	4
8	168	153	3
9	427	390	4
TOTAL	3619	3309	36

3619YD · 3309M · PAR 36

fail to match your handicap. The courses cover a broad area with plenty of elevation change; renting a golf cart is advisable.

There are many memorable holes. The 6th on the Lake nine is a great par 4. From the back, it plays 441yd/403m downhill with the fairway narrowing between a copse of trees and a large lateral bunker. The hole is made by the second shot, across a lake that continues in front of the large, sloping green angled away right. This is a relatively easy five but a very difficult par. On the toughest nine, Valley, the 2nd to the 5th holes are truly demanding, particularly the 2nd – 538yd/492m across two water carries to a steep, elevated green flanking the lake (see p.18).

The vast clubhouse, looking like a cruise liner beached on the hillside, offers spectacular

Above: Reaching the green of the par 4 3rd (Valley) requires a long accurate second to clear protective water. Below: The elevated green of the uphill 3rd (Lake) has large bunkers and water along the right.

views, even from the very luxurious changing rooms. With 11,960 sq yd/10,000 sq m of space, it offers considerable amenities. The Rom Pho restaurant, in addition to a panoramic view, offers Thai, Japanese and European menus and can seat 400 diners. There is also a snack bar, a members' lounge with a piano bar, a substantial pro-shop, wine cellar, snooker tables, a fitness centre and complete convention facilities. Next to the clubhouse is a 40-room Golf Lodge, for comfortable on-course accommodation.

Treasure Hill

Treasure Hill Golf & Country Club, 222 Moo 7,
Klongkuew District, Banbung, Chonburi 20220
TEL: *(038) 420 766, (01) 344 8002*
FAX: *(038) 420 767*
LOCATION: *Km 76 on Route 331*
COURSE: *18 holes, 7241yd/6621m, par 72*
TYPE OF COURSE: *Gently sloping parkland with*
mountain views
DESIGNER: *Yoshikazu Kato (1997)*
GREEN FEES: *B*
FACILITIES: *Golf shop, caddies, cart and equipment*
hire, shoe and umbrella rental, putting green, changing
facilities, Japanese bath, refreshment shelters on course,
restaurant in clubhouse
VISITORS: *Soft spikes only*

This is definitely a place to play – for the location and setting, if nothing else. Treasure Hill lives up to its name. It is a relatively new members' club, open to visitors and laid out in an extremely attractive situation. Backed on several sides by rising, heavily wooded hills, the clubhouse sits above sloping land, giving a view out over the whole course. The course was designed by Yoshikazu Kato, creator of the two courses at Blue Canyon in Phuket. It falls away in a series of plateaux and levels to a wooded valley beyond. This is a highly strategic layout, with a good variety of mature trees left in situ. It is very much a golfer's course, with large trees in the line of play, deep man-made chasms and water hazards (no doubt borrowing on the Blue Canyon experience), good greens and sensational views. Placing your shots is critical here; you cannot always see the sand and water. The course plays fairly long, and the fairways suffer somewhat from the encroachment of local grass, but the doglegs are gentle and the excellent greens have plenty of movement to keep you on your toes. The natural levels and plateaux give the course considerable interest. The clubhouse is small, casual, unpretentious and very welcoming. This course is still relatively unknown, but it is not to be missed.

Below: The course falls away down the hill from the
clubhouse, with the 18th green in the foreground.

Pattaya Country Club

Pattaya Country Club & Resort, 31 Moo 2, Khao Mai Khaw, Banglamung, Chonburi 20150
TEL: *(038) 423 718-9* **FAX:** *(038) 423 718-9*
LOCATION: *3km before Route 36 junction on Route 331*
COURSE: *18 holes, 6775yd/6195m, par 72*
TYPE OF COURSE: *Gently undulating open land with newly planted trees and some water hazards*
DESIGNER: *Virayuth Phetbuasak and Peter Rehn (1995)*
GREEN FEES: *BB*
FACILITIES: *Golf shop, caddies, cart and golf equipment hire, shoe and umbrella rental, driving range, putting green, changing facilities, refreshment shelters on course, restaurant in clubhouse*
VISITORS: *Welcome, but advance telephone call advised*

This is a pleasant, gently undulating course that offers all the elements required for the holiday golfer, without placing too many demands on his or her skill. A course, in other words, that higher handicaps will enjoy. There are broad, level fairways that run up and over a central hill and not too many severe hazards. The design, or rather lack of it, has provided some fairly unadventurous holes, too many blind shots and a number of concealed hazards that do not worry a player since they are not in view. On the credit side, the course is kept in fine shape, with good greens and nice little clumps of flowering shrubs around the tees. The pleasant views of distant hills, however, are somewhat marred by a number of large electric pylons straddling the site, but which, fortunately, are not in play.

Not too far inland from Pattaya town, this is an inexpensive, perfectly playable course in a setting of green space, gentle slopes, palm trees and limited water. The back nine, locally redesigned, provides more interest, particularly the 16th, a 179-yd/164-m par 3. This is played across a lake left to a green tilted towards you (and the water) encircled by sand. There is, perhaps surprisingly, an attractive and well-equipped driving range.

Below: Gentle slopes, shallow mounded bunkers and broad fairways provide very playable golf.

Siam Country Club

*Siam Country Club, 50 Moo 9, Tambol Poeng,
Banglamung, Chonburi 20150*
TEL: *(038) 249 381-6* **FAX:** *(038) 249 387*
LOCATION: *Route 3 to Km 36 marker, left to Route
36. Course after 9km*
COURSE: *18 holes, 7016yd/6415m, par 72*
TYPE OF COURSE: *Well-established parkland course
sloping across a river valley with many mature trees*
DESIGNER: *I. Izumi (1971)*
GREEN FEES: *B*
FACILITIES: *Golf shop, caddies, cart and golf equipment
hire, shoe rental, driving range, putting green, changing
facilities, accommodation on-site, swimming pool,
snooker, games and fitness room, refreshment shelters on
course, restaurant in clubhouse*
VISITORS: *Welcome, but advance booking necessary*

This is the second-oldest of the post-war
resort golf courses and the first created by
private enterprise. For nearly 20 years, along
with the Tourist Association course at
Bangpra, Siam Country Club was the venue
of choice for those seeking weekend relief
from the heat and pollution of Bangkok, with
on-site accommodation and attendant
facilities. The excellent design of this course,

by I. Izumi of Japan, has withstood the test of
time. With the mature growth of the
many trees lining the holes, it still represents
an excellent challenge. Four Thailand
Opens were played here between 1973 and
1984, as well as the Ladies Thailand Open
in 1984.

From the multilevel clubhouse, below a
hilltop Chinese Buddha, the course flows
down to a transverse watercourse, which forms
the primary hazard on six holes. It then climbs
gently uphill on the far side, its fairways flanked
with tall palms and other species, including red
flushes of flowering jacaranda and quaintly
sculpted animal and bird topiary. The fairways
have local, broad-bladed grass and the greens
remain slow, despite modern technology.
However, as a test of golf, this is still among
the best in the country and is good value for
money. The best holes are the 15th and 17th,
each a dogleg where water plays a key role.

*Below: Putting on the elevated green of the par 5 18th, a
tough uphill dogleg left.*

10  Phoenix

Phoenix Golf and Country Club, Km 158, Sukhumvit Road, Huayyai, Banglamung, Chonburi 20260
TEL: *(038) 239 391-8* **FAX:** *(038) 239 402*
LOCATION: *Km 158 Route 3, approximately 12km south of Pattaya*
COURSE: *27 holes: Mountain 3449yd/3154m; Lakes 3261yd/2982m; Ocean 3363yd/3075m; all par 36*
TYPE OF COURSE: *Undulating parkland flowing downhill from elevated site with mature trees and some strategic water*
DESIGNER: *Dennis Griffiths (1993)*
GREEN FEES: *BB*
FACILITIES: *Golf shop, caddies, cart and golf equipment hire, shoe and umbrella rental, driving range, putting green, changing facilities, tennis, swimming pool, snooker, games and television room, children's playroom, refreshment shelters on course, restaurant in clubhouse*
VISITORS: *Welcome, but advance booking necessary. Only four players allowed per group*

The best part of Phoenix is the view, especially from the vast bronze-roofed atrium of the clubhouse, which would dwarf many hotels. From this vantage point, the 27-hole course eases along and down a hillside, offering distant views of the high-rises of Pattaya and the ocean, pastel shades of craggy mountain peaks and numerous temples puncturing the treeline on the horizon. Constructed at the peak of Thailand's period of golfing expansion, a number of grand plans have clearly gone on hold, but there is plenty of golf to play.

The course was an early effort by Dennis Griffiths, who went on to design the magnificent layouts of Thai Country Club and Soi Dao Highland. The three nines run over a sizeable tract of land, offering spacious and relatively undemanding golf. The driving areas are friendly, the mounding gentle and the bunkers large but shallow. There are a sprinkling of trees, too few to seriously affect play. The land itself, with its rolling natural slopes, creates much of the interest on the three courses, where the yardages are comparatively comfortable.

Below: Water and much sand to carry, backed by views of temples and distant mountain peaks.

Rayong Green Valley

Rayong Green Valley Country Club, 23 Moo 7, Ban Chang, Rayong 21130
TEL: *(038) 893 300-5* **FAX:** *(038) 893 754*
LOCATION: *5km north of Ban Chang, Route 3376*
COURSE: *18 holes, 7264yd/6642m, par 72*
TYPE OF COURSE: *Gently undulating parkland with mature palms flowing through a river valley*
DESIGNER: *Peter W. Thomson and Michael Wolveridge (1992)*
GREEN FEES: *BB*
FACILITIES: *Golf shop, caddies, cart and golf equipment hire, shoe and umbrella rental, putting green, changing facilities, refreshment shelters on course, restaurant in clubhouse*
VISITORS: *Welcome, but advance telephone call advised*

RAYONG GREEN VALLEY

HOLE	YD	M	PAR	HOLE	YD	M	PAR
1	560	512	5	10	396	362	4
2	185	169	3	11	590	539	5
3	384	351	4	12	150	137	3
4	594	543	5	13	445	407	4
5	437	400	4	14	462	422	4
6	429	392	4	15	473	432	4
7	388	355	4	16	179	164	3
8	560	512	5	17	390	357	4
9	235	215	3	18	417	381	4
OUT	3760	3438	36	IN	3504	3204	36

7264YD • 6642M • PAR 72

This is part of the Green Valley group, which manages five courses in Thailand, and the only one that lives up to its name. Laid out along the slopes of a gentle river valley, this is a fine first effort in the country by the design team of Michael Wolveridge and five-times British Open Champion Peter W Thomson. It represents all that relaxed, intelligent holiday golf should be – a course designed with subtlety and restraint, working with rather than against nature. Broad and gently undulating fairways follow the shape of the land past tall casurinas, varieties of palm and even cacti. Gently mounded, visible bunkers lead to natural indigenous rough. Good use has been made of the attractive watercourses with jumbled boulders and a blaze of colourful flowers enhancing each hole, yet in no way interfering with play. The undoubted charm lies in the very natural aspect of the layout;

the holes seem always to have been there, waiting to be displayed by the designer. Even the distance markers are formed from clumps of bushes and rock. This is a genuinely peaceful location, with golf to delight the eye and cleanse the soul.

The holes – most of which run over sloping, undulating land– are nicely framed by mature trees and distant mountain peaks. The most interesting stretch, and in many ways the most typical, follows the river valley in the front nine. The 7th is a sharp dogleg left,

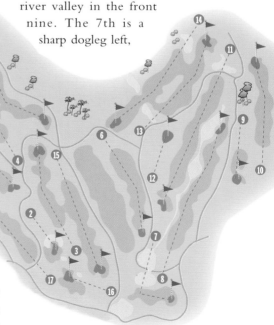

Above: Very floral and attractive, the 12th hole is short but hazardous, with water below right.

tempting the big hitters with a long water carry. The 560-yd/512-m 8th hole meanders deceptively uphill, winding along the water on the left. Then, after two typical Thomson links–style holes across a sloping hillside, players return to the river valley for the 11th hole, a fine 590-yd/539-m downhill par 5. There is water and rough to carry from the tee, a sinuous fairway where the left-hand creek nudges in at intervals and, providing you have been long enough to get there, an approach across another water hazard to a small green protected by sand. This is exciting stuff, designed to be played within one's capability.

Green Valley recently opened a further 18 holes, grandly titled St Andrews 2000, and a fine new clubhouse, serving both courses. This new layout by Desmond Muirhead is in complete contrast, running over rugged, often severely sloping land with some huge water carries and impenetrable rough. It boasts two par 6 holes (855yd/781m and 857yd/784m respectively), an excessive green fee and a scorecard warning to 'take enough golf balls and … to ensure your safety, lost balls should not be searched for'. A definite golfing challenge, probably unplayable by the majority – but the 'Home of Golf' it is not.

THAI TRANSPORT

Most major towns are linked by air or rail, but local transport is by road. In Bangkok, taxis abound (look for 'Taxi Meter', although you must bargain late at night). Elsewhere, buses (non-air-conditioned) or a '5-baht bus' (a converted pickup truck) follow scheduled routes. Alternatively, there is the ubiquitous *tuk-tuk*, (three-wheeled, cramped and noisy), motorcycle taxis (one rides on the pillion) or the leisurely two-seater *samlaw*, powered by an ageing cyclist.

Eastern Star

*Eastern Star Country Club, 241/5 Moo 3, Banchang,
Rayong 21130*
TEL: *(038) 630 410-17* **FAX:** *(038) 630 418*
LOCATION: *Take Route 3 to Km 193 marker; course
approximately 2km from Banchang*
COURSE: *18 holes, 7134yd/6523m, par 72*
TYPE OF COURSE: *Gently undulating course lined
with mounded palms and good use of sand and water*
DESIGNER: *Robert Trent Jones Jr (1992)*
GREEN FEES: *BB*
FACILITIES: *Golf shop, caddies, cart and golf equipment
hire, shoe and umbrella rental, driving range, putting
green, changing facilities, sauna, swimming pool, tennis
courts, beach pool, fitness centre, refreshment shelters on
course, bar and restaurant in clubhouse*
VISITORS: *Welcome, but advance telephone call
recommended*

EASTERN STAR

HOLE	YD	M	PAR	HOLE	YD	M	PAR
1	421	385	4	10	415	379	4
2	596	545	5	11	449	410	4
3	327	299	4	12	203	186	3
4	167	153	3	13	577	528	5
5	417	381	4	14	390	357	4
6	532	486	5	15	193	176	3
7	451	412	4	16	421	385	4
8	206	188	3	17	509	465	5
9	415	379	4	18	445	407	4
OUT	3532	3230	36	IN	3602	3294	36

7134YD • 6523M • PAR 72

A firm favourite with many, Eastern Star manages to be all things to all people. Essentially a members' club, it also welcomes visitors and has excellent facilities within what is clearly a golf club environment. The clubhouse, although fairly substantial, is strictly functional. From the spacious, friendly ground floor bar and restaurant (the locker rooms, somewhat unusually, are upstairs, near the entrance) players step straight out onto the course, close to the 1st and 10th tees.

This is a well-established layout by experienced American Robert Trent Jones Jr and reflects his policy of creating courses that are highly playable by the average golfer from the members' tees, but offer a much sterner test from the back. The holes follow gently undulating, in places sloping, land, with fairly wide, subtly contoured fairways and large areas of penal water affecting two-thirds of them. Stands of tall coconut trees, often on large, rolling mounds, form an attractive backdrop, while the bunkers are large, well defined and relatively shallow. Do not expect the highest standards of manicuring at what is a relatively inexpensive facility. With mango trees and splashes of floral colour, this is a very pleasant place to test your game and an excellent choice for the holiday golfer visiting this area.

Recently, the course has reversed the order of the two nines, providing a much more demanding finish. The 17th is a 509-yd/465-m par 5 off the back tee, all uphill and highly strategic. In what is essentially a double dogleg, the drive has to be placed in a narrow neck between two sets of fairway bunkers, while avoiding two lakes right and, for big hitters, another large lake straight ahead. The hole then widens to the right, around the lake, before demanding an approach to a semi-island green ringed by sand and water. Negotiate that and the last has more water and even more sand. The fairway on this 445-yd/407-m par 4 bends narrowly past water on both sides and large bunkers before offering an approach to a semi-blind sunken green, surrounded by sweeping mounds and much sand.

The club has good practice facilities, including a driving range named The Birdie Factory. In the restaurant, there is a fine menu, featuring both Thai and international dishes, and a good selection of wine at reasonable prices. Golf and business can go hand-in-hand. On-site is a large resort and

Above: Looking towards the sunken 18th green and clubhouse. Below: The approach to the sloping 10th green needs to avoid the water lurking right.

executive conference centre with meeting rooms and accommodation in the adjacent well-furnished Golf Villas. Other facilities include a swimming pool, a beach pool, four floodlit tennis courts and a fitness centre.

13 Soi Dao Highland

*Soi Dao Highland Golf Club & Resort, 153/1 Moo 2,
Tambol Tabsai, Pong Nam Ron, Chanthaburi 22140*
TEL:*(039) 322 831-2, 387 123* **FAX:** *(039) 321
483*
LOCATION: *Off Route 317 to Chanthaburi at Km 41*
COURSE: *18 holes, 7162yd/6549m, par 72*
TYPE OF COURSE: *Sloping parkland in a mountain
setting*
DESIGNER: *Dennis Griffiths (1995)*
GREEN FEES: *BB*
FACILITIES: *Golf shop, caddies, cart and golf equipment
hire, shoe and umbrella rental, driving range, putting
green, changing facilities, refreshment facilities on course,
restaurant in clubhouse, adjacent hotel, karaoke, Jacuzzi,
sauna, watersports, bicycles*
VISITORS: *Welcome, but advance telephone call
suggested*

SOI DAO HIGHLAND							
HOLE	YD	M	PAR	HOLE	YD	M	PAR
1	438	400	4	10	419	383	4
2	348	318	4	11	469	429	4
3	206	188	3	12	201	184	3
4	552	505	5	13	433	396	4
5	223	204	3	14	399	365	4
6	476	435	4	15	583	533	5
7	364	333	4	16	169	154	3
8	528	483	5	17	391	358	4
9	430	393	4	18	533	487	5
OUT	3565	3260	36	IN	3597	3289	36

7162YD • 6549M • PAR 72

This is almost certainly the most dramatic
and beautiful location for golf in Thailand. Below the towering majesty of Soi Dao
Mountain, one of the country's highest peaks,
the course flows past ancient trees, untouched
rainforest, placid lakes and a riot of flora. An
escapist's dream and, with a comfortable resort
hotel on site, a very popular weekend retreat
from Bangkok. Situated a little north of
Chanthaburi close to the Cambodian border,
this course combines the charm of its forested
mountain setting with an excellent, highly
playable test of golf.

Dennis Griffiths, whose
Thailand portfolio includes
the Thai Country Club,
Dynasty, Chiangmai Green
Valley and Phoenix, was
provided with a dream
location on which to exercise his
talents. To his credit, he has left
many of the tall, age-old trees as
key features on several holes, some
alongside an untouched green
screen of virgin jungle. The course,
immaculately groomed with trim
shrubbery, flowering trees in white
and yellow plus vivid flamboyants,

stands out in dramatic verdant contrast to the
untamed wilderness beyond its borders. It
flows up and over a series of hills, with rarely
a level lie, creating interesting strategic
choices and the pleasure of an amazing vista
round every corner. The architect has allowed
the sloping mountain foothills to dictate play,
blending his art into the ageless pattern of
nature. The result is as close as one may come
to golfing heaven, in the same elevated
perfection as Pevero in Sardinia, Bali Handara
or Santo da Serra in Madeira. It is a haven of
peace and

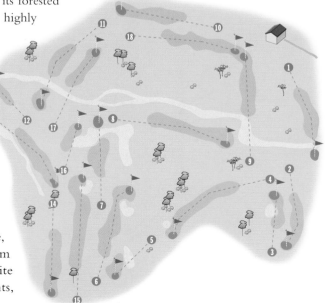

*Above: Downhill 3rd with superb views over the clubhouse/
hotel. Below: Teeshot view of the demanding par 4 11th.*

tranquillity, backed by the insistent chorus of
nature and a fine test of golf for anyone.

Where water appears, it is highly strategic
and puts a premium on confident club
selection. Particularly at the par 4 11th
(469yd/429m), one of the great holes, where
the narrow downhill teeshot is to a fairway
turning left round tall trees. With a fairway
bunker dead on line, the hole then cuts back
right round a dense wood, with the second
shot having to carry a strategic, hidden creek
before reaching the green (see photo right).

Every hole is a delight, each offering its
own individual examination as the course
cascades greenly around the mountain slopes.
There are many memories – caddies in blue
and black with straw hats; mangos hanging
from a lakeside tree at the 4th; a stone-built
drinks shelter nestling into the jungle fringe
behind the 12th; reaching the elevated 10th
green to find a large crystal lake and Soi Dao

mountain beyond – above all, a sense of
peaceful isolation and proximity to nature.

The hotel, by the clubhouse with a
panoramic view over the course, has very
comfortable rooms. Future plans include a
'bet-settling' short 19th hole plus a further
nine.

Caddie Culture

Thailand's greatest gifts to golf are the myriad caddies who populate every golf club. They are almost always female, smiling, helpful and extremely knowledgeable. In colourful numbered uniforms, different for each club, these well-trained women are there to advise and help you to enjoy your round to the full. Despite the variation in green fees throughout the country, all caddies will pull your clubs (or ride on your golf cart) over 18 holes for the price of a top-grade golf ball back home.

On arrival at the club, your caddie will take your bag and check the number of clubs (and recheck after the round). After you have hit a couple of shots, she will have a shrewd idea of your ability, but will normally tell you the yardage rather than club unless you ask. She will also fill in your divots, will mark and clean your ball on the green, give you the correct putting line, meticulously keep your score on a card and generally do her best to make the round *sanuk* (fun). Many caddies will line up the lettering on your ball along the correct putting line; others will perhaps suggest 'two balls right, uphill'. Either way, trust her and remember that she sees these greens every day and knows them better than you ever will, particularly when assessing the effect of grain. Thai caddies are a welcome breath of fresh air in the world of golf. In addition to their highly professional and informed approach, they will genuinely want you to enjoy yourself and score the best you can. The language of golf is universal and you will be surprised how her enthusiastic support can improve your game.

After the round, your caddie may well clean your shoes as well as your clubs. Tip her well (around 200 baht) – she will have earned it. Also, remember her at the drinks stops on the way round – it's hot caddying as well as playing. Above all, enjoy the experience.

REGIONAL DIRECTORY

Where to Stay
Pattaya
Royal Cliff Beach Resort (038 250 421-40, Fax: 038 250 511) Set in secluded clifftop gardens south of town, this elegant resort has four hotels catering to four distinct lifestyles. The Beach Hotel is popular, lively and excellent value; the Grand lives up to its name, with sweeping ocean views and superb facilities. The Cliff Terrace offers verdant low-rise seclusion near the beach, while the Royal Wing – its suites-only accommodation overlooking the bay and a private, free-form pool – is the ultimate in luxury, with private butler service. Nine very individual restaurants, four bars and a new spa head a complete range of leisure and sports facilities. The resort also has its own catamaran for visitors wishing to spend a day island-hopping.

Dusit Resort (038 425 611-7, Fax: 038 428 239) High on a private promontory overlooking the sea just north of the main beach and the town, the hotel maintains the Dusit reputation for quality and service. The 460 rooms are attractively appointed and complemented by a choice of Chinese, southern European and international dining in three restaurants. Guests can choose between bar lounges, with live evening music, two magnificent swimming pools, three floodlit tennis courts and a comprehensive fitness centre that also offers traditional Thai massage.

Cholcham Pattaya Resort (038 702 777, Fax: 038 702 778) This hotel is located a little north of town (there is a regular hotel minibus transfer). One of the main features of this friendly hotel is its attractive landscaped gardens running down past the popular swimming pool and Jacuzzi to the edge of a secluded sandy beach. Guests can choose between Western and Asian specialities in the coffee shop, a Vietnamese restaurant or fresh seafood barbecued under the tall garden palms near the pool. There is a fitness centre, tennis and squash facilities plus sauna and massage.

Sriracha
The City Hotel (038 322 700, Fax: 038 322 740) As its name implies, this hotel is right in the heart of Sriracha town. It is therefore handy for shopping and centrally located for some dozen of the excellent golf courses north of Pattaya. This hotel is very popular with Japanese business people and golfers, not least for the Shiki Japanese restaurant, noted for its traditional and very authentic cuisine. An international menu is available in the coffee shop; there is also a bar lounge and coffee corner. Fitness addicts will favour the pool or the Clark Hatch fitness centre alongside.

Where to Eat
In this region, where 28 golf courses are spread out over a fairly extensive area, all roads lead to Pattaya and its myriad pleasures. These include a wide choice of dining out. The excellent range of large international hotels along the seafront offers a selection of restaurants. One fine example is the **Marco Polo** in the Montien (038 428 155), where Hong Kong chefs prepare authentic Chinese specialities. Other choices are **La Gritta** at the Amari Orchid (038 428 161) for Italian and seafood or **Mai Kai Supper Club** at the Tropicana (038 428 645) for atmospheric Polynesian food. For a genuine touch of class, pay a visit to **Bruno's** (038 361 073) and be assured of gourmet dining and fine wines in an elegant candlelit setting. For fresh fish and seafood, sample the **Lobster Pot** (038 426 083), perched out on a jetty over the sea for an authentic maritime atmosphere. Beef lovers will appreciate the **El Toro Steak House** (038 426 239), where only their own aged and seasoned beef is available. As an alternative, the **Captain's Corner Steak House** (038 364 318) has an all-you-can-eat seafood and steak barbecue, seats over 100 and offers courtesy transport from and to your hotel. For Thai food, try the **Sugar Hut Restaurant** (038 251 686), which echoes the Ayutthaya period, or **PIC Kitchen** (038 428 374), which offers classical Thai dining in four wooden garden pavilions. **Ruen Thai** (038 425 911) combines Thai food with an evening classical show. For something completely different, have the seafood buffet lunch or dinner on the 52nd and 53rd floor revolving restaurants of the **Pattaya Park Tower** (038 251 201-8) on nearby Jomtien Beach.

What to See
In what is a comparatively new area for tourism, sightseeing is more of the man-made variety than historical. However, anyone interested in the religion of Thailand should visit **Wat Yan Sangwararam**. This is a collection of Thai temples built in the styles of many dynasties and nations, including Burmese, Indian and Chinese, all set around a peaceful lake. Garden fanciers will want to visit the **Nong Nooch** tropical village and orchid farm, which has beautiful gardens, a cactus house, a small zoo and daily cultural show. For wildlife, one can choose between the **Elephant Village**, the **Pattaya Crocodile Farm**, both with daily shows, the **Khao Keow Open Zoo** and the **Sriracha Tiger Farm**, with the world's largest collection of tigers in captivity. Also, take in one of the truly spectacular transvestite shows, at **Alcazar** (038 429 694) or **Tiffany** (038 421 700-3).

Chapter 3

Saraburi Region

Of the seven regions covered in this book, this is probably the least known as a tourist destination. Reachable in a little over two hours travelling north-east from Bangkok, its primary claim to fame is as a getaway destination for nature-loving Thais escaping the city over the weekend. Largely undeveloped and punctuated by craggy mountains, their slopes shrouded in cascades of tropical trees and verdant flora, the area offers an attractive combination of peaceful farms and fruit orchards with nature in the raw. It is Thailand's main area for dairy cattle and is home to the oldest national wildlife park in the country. It also serves as the gateway to the kingdom's largest topographical region – I-san (the north-east) – a vast, fairly arid plateau

bounded on its northern and eastern boundaries with neighbouring Laos by the Mekong River and in the south by the Dongrak mountains bordering Cambodia. Although there are nearly 30 golf courses throughout the north-east, the concentration of several modern layouts near to the town of Saraburi has created a genuine resort golfing destination.

Golf is a fairly recent arrival in this region. Apart from a couple of rustic courses that are no longer in play, the development of golf here dates only from 1992. Before that, this green and fertile area supported farming. The bulk of Thailand's dairy produce comes from here. Around Muaklek and Pak Chong you are in 'cowboy country'. Steak-house restaurants abound along with ranch-style resorts, and horse riding offers opportunities to explore the dramatic hinterland.

Left: Spectacular waterfalls are a feature in Khao Yai.
Above: An exotic market fruit display.

Close by lies the Khao Yai National Park, the oldest and third-largest in Thailand. Designated a national park in 1962, it is spread over 2168 sq km/837 sq miles of mountainous wilderness. It offers some of the richest diversity of flora and fauna in Asia. Although there is adequate road access and the opportunity to follow some 50km/31 miles of nature trails, much of the land is virgin rainforest, home to a wide variety of protected species – more than enough for any nature lover. More than 320 species of exotic birdlife, including four varieties of hornbill (one of the largest tropical forest birds) live undisturbed in the primal environment. The park is also home to the wild elephant, tiger (rarely seen) and leopard, barking deer, sambar, pig-tailed

macaque and white-handed gibbon. Some species may be observed – particularly at dusk – others are merely heard. The park is also home to black bear, slow loris, wild dogs, hog badgers, porcupines, giant squirrels, python, Siamese cobras, monitor lizards and green tree vipers, among others. For the city dweller, this opportunity to observe wildlife in its natural jungle habitat, unfenced and independent, is a rare treat indeed. There are wildlife-watching towers, observable salt licks and spotlit tours each evening. There are bat caves and a number of spectacular waterfalls, the largest of which is Haew Narok (Hell Waterfall), which plunges 150m/492ft in three stages. The Royal Forest Department maintains restaurant and information areas in four locations.

For the visitor interested in the history and cultural diversity of Thailand, exploring the rural charm of I-san can

Below: From elevated viewing platforms, truly magnificent vistas of verdant hills across the Khao Yai National Park can be appreciated.

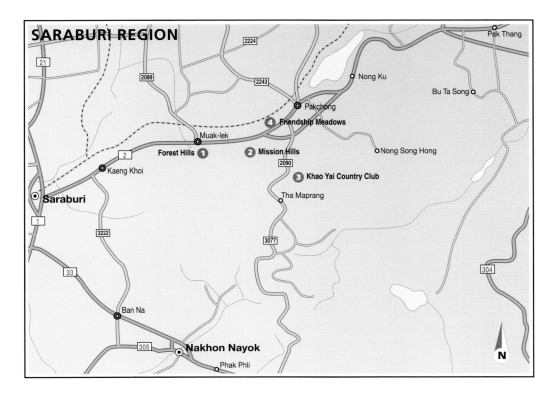

SARABURI REGION

Pak Thang

21

2224

2089

2243

Nong Ku

Bu Ta Song

Pakchong

Friendship Meadows 4

Muak-lek

Forest Hills 1   Mission Hills 2   Nong Song Hong

2   2090

Kaeng Khoi

Khao Yai Country Club 3

Saraburi

Tha Maprang

1

3222

3077

33   304

Ban Na

305   Nakhon Nayok

Phak Phli

N

prove rewarding. With an economy based almost entirely on agriculture, life has changed little and the colourful local culture, closely linked to the land and seasons, can be enjoyed through festivals, dance and spicy cuisine. Three notable events are the Bang Fai festival in May, when giant homemade rockets are fired to encourage rainfall, parades of large, elaborate beeswax candles and castles in July and October, and the November Elephant Roundup in Surin. Handmade textiles flourish, in particular the famous *matmi* silk, which is made from tie-dyed yarn.

The region also offers prehistoric pottery and rock paintings at 5000-year-old sites near Khorat and Khong Chiam, plus some of the finest examples of ancient Khmer temples outside Cambodia. The best of these is the 12th-century complex at Phimai, some 60km/37 miles north of Nakhon Ratchasima. Not too far away in Buri Ram province, the 10th-century temple at Prasat Phanom Rung has fine carvings.

TEMPLE TREASURES

Phimai Historical Park contains the largest collection of Khmer buildings in Thailand, which underlines its significance as the gateway to the Khmer Kingdom to the south. Carefully restored, this temple complex was built during the reign of King Jayavarman II in the 12th century. Traces can still be seen of the ancient city and the road that once linked it to Angkor Wat in Cambodia. The complex is also home to the world's largest banyan tree and a museum that features treasures and art from the golden age of the Khmer, as well as housing many examples of prehistoric remains found in the region.

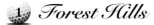

Forest Hills

Sir James Resort and Forest Hills Country Club, 195 Moo 3, Mittrapharb Road, Tambol Mittrapharb, Amphur Muak-lek, Saraburi 18180
TEL: *(036) 341 911-4* **FAX:** *(036) 341 957*
EMAIL: *sirjames@ksc.th.com*
LOCATION: *Km 141 marker, Muak-lek*
COURSE: *18 holes, 7026yd/6424m, par 72*
TYPE OF COURSE: *Pure parkland in a forested mountain setting*
DESIGNER: *Veerayuth Phetbuasak (1993)*
GREEN FEES: *BB*
FACILITIES: *Golf shop, caddies, cart and golf equipment hire, shoe and umbrella rental, driving range, putting green, changing facilities, sauna, Jacuzzi, swimming pool, snooker, accommodation on site, restaurants in clubhouse, refreshment shelters on course*
VISITORS: *Welcome, but an advance telephone call advised*

FOREST HILLS

HOLE	YD	M	PAR	HOLE	YD	M	PAR
1	483	442	4	10	555	507	5
2	356	325	4	11	206	188	3
3	533	487	5	12	380	348	4
4	180	164	3	13	445	407	4
5	450	411	4	14	560	512	5
6	203	186	3	15	164	150	3
7	450	411	4	16	400	366	4
8	542	496	5	17	368	336	4
9	365	333	4	18	386	353	4
OUT	3562	3257	36	IN	3464	3168	36

7026YD • 6424M • PAR 72

This is probably the most complete and attractively situated leisure resort with golf in all Thailand. Just two hours' drive north-east of Bangkok into mountain country near the Khao Yai National Park, the club is something of an undiscovered gem for visitors. Yet, with its well-established infrastructure and excellent amenities, it has much to offer holidaymakers.

The location is idyllic. There is a large hilltop clubhouse and resort lodge buildings offering superb views out over the slopes and plateaux of the golf course, all surrounded by densely wooded mountains. Whichever way you turn, the outlook is enchanting. With mature woodland, chalet-style houses and fields with cattle, there is an old-fashioned feel to the beautiful setting. Apart from the climate, you could imagine yourself in Switzerland. The resort was the brainchild of the late Sir James Holt, an expatriate Englishman who bought a dairy farm in the centre of Thailand's beef and dairy country, and later decided to turn it into a golf course. Avoiding the lure of imported international golf course construction, the resort has created a course in pure British parkland style, backed by a charming mountain setting.

The land has largely been allowed to define and shape the holes; the wealth of mature trees creating a parkland atmosphere. What the course may lack in design sophistication, it more than makes up for in the array of attractive flowers, neat little hedges, casual clumps of cypress, coconut palm and rocks and tall casurina trees. Overall, careful manicuring makes the course neat and tidy, without intruding on what is essentially a holiday resort golf course.

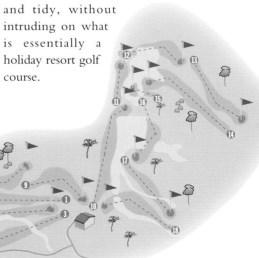

The holes play quite long off the back tees, but noticeably more comfortably from the tees of the day. However, it is the often the quite severely sloping land that presents the main challenge. There are a number of areas of strategic water and bunkers unusually raked up to the lip or the edge of the green. The well-maintained greens are fairly level despite the hilly surroundings.

There are many memorable holes, with sloping, sometimes tilted fairways. Probably the best on the front nine is the 7th. This is a severe dogleg left par 4, played over a blind crest. A long drive with draw yields dividends, if it manages to avoid a small water hazard on the corner below. The green is uphill on a well-defended plateau. The final four holes, all involving water, changes of elevation and precise placement from the tee, provide a good test for any player.

Below: At the long par 3 11th, water beckons magnetically all along the right-hand side.

BUDDHISM

Buddhism is one of the two pillars of Thai society and culture, the other being the monarchy. Buddhism is practised by 95 per cent of the population. Elegantly decorated *wats* (temples) are a focal point of every town or village, and the religion and the 250,000 monks who represent it are a very visible part of daily life. In saffron robes, the monks act as teachers, mediators and officiate at weddings, funerals and a variety of public events. People present daily food and gifts to the monks as a means of earning merit. At some point in their youth, most men live temporarily in a monastery for their spiritual development.

The Lodge, adjacent to the clubhouse, has 84 comfortable rooms with cable/satellite television, all offering superb views over the course and the distant mountains. There is also a fitness centre, beauty salon and, for non-golfers, tennis, riding, shooting and fishing.

② *Mission Hills*

Mission Hills Golf Club & Resort, 151 Moo 5, Mhoosee, Pakchong, Nakhon Ratchasima 30130
TEL: *(02) 551 9030-1* **FAX:** *(02) 551 9081*
LOCATION: *30km south of Pakchong; Route 2090 or via Haew Plakang Road from Route 2*
COURSE: *18 holes, 7058yd/6454m, par 72*
TYPE OF COURSE: *Well-landscaped international championship course laid out over rolling land surrounded by mountains*
DESIGNER: *Jack Nicklaus (1993)*
GREEN FEES: *BB*
FACILITIES: *Golf shop, caddies, cart and golf equipment hire, shoe and umbrella rental, driving range, putting green, changing facilities, accommodation on site, swimming pool, snooker, sauna, mountain bike, coffee shop in clubhouse*
VISITORS: *Welcome, but advance reservation required*

MISSION HILLS							
HOLE	YD	M	PAR	HOLE	YD	M	PAR
1	408	373	4	10	438	400	4
2	508	464	5	11	198	181	3
3	442	404	4	12	535	489	5
4	208	190	3	13	383	350	4
5	549	502	5	14	472	431	4
6	403	368	4	15	174	159	3
7	359	328	4	16	407	372	4
8	176	161	3	17	388	355	4
9	438	400	4	18	572	523	5
OUT	3491	3192	36	IN	3567	3262	36

7058 YD • 6454M • PAR 72

Of the five courses designed by Jack Nicklaus in Thailand, this one undoubtedly has the most dramatic and scenic location. It is one of two golf properties operated by the same company (the other is also called Mission Hills, and is situated near Kanchanaburi). Laid out on two sides of a large hill, most of the holes are set on a rolling plateau surrounded by spectacular, wooded crags. As a setting in which to play golf, it is quite amazing. There are views of distant peaks that blend in with the lush tropical surroundings to distract you from your game, and even echoes of China in the landscape.

This is a resort development that was clearly planned on a grand scale, but which suffered during Thailand's economic slowdown, especially with real estate sales. The clubhouse/hotel is palatial, with a vast marbled entrance hall that seems out of place in such a location, particularly at a golf resort. The under-used facilities are a testimony to a lavish master plan that has so far been unfulfilled.

The golf course itself, however, is first-class and maintained in excellent condition. In comparison with many of the Nicklaus courses created in holiday locations, this is a very fair design for average players, particularly if they use their heads in shot selection.

The course follows the lie of the land; the first hole and the final 12 flow over an undulating plateau in the shadow of several steep, wooded mountains. The other five, somewhat disconcertingly, are reached by travelling over a saddle between two large hills and are quite separate from the rest. The bunkers, filled with a deep ochre-coloured sand, are well positioned but clearly visible. The Tifdwarf greens have an even speed and relatively little movement. Mastering this

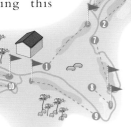

course is all about playing from a tee that is within your reach and playing nominated, well-positioned drives to leave a less demanding approach.

After the opening hole, there is some distance to go before reaching the 2nd tee on the other side of a steep hill. These 'other' holes, although highly strategic, lack the dramatic surroundings of the main course. This starts again at the 7th, a short par 4 of 359yd/328m made by the quite fantastic location (see photo right). Off the tee, you have a choice – to play driver onto a higher level left, carrying two cross bunkers in the centre of this split fairway, or to play for position down the right and then have an approach across sand to a narrow, undulating green. This hole is followed by the short 8th, (see photo below) all carry over water to an

angled green backed by sand. The further the pin is to the right, the greater the water carry and the shallower the target. A testing shot, not helped by the definite distraction of the sensational view. From here, the course flows over and across an undulating plateau flanked by steeply rising wooded hills. With few trees, some water and much sand, this is a course to savour in a superlative setting.

Above: Superb views on the par 4 7th hole.
Below: Visual distractions at the short 8th, which requires precise club selection.

Khao Yai Country Club

The Country Club Khao-Yai, Km 23, Thanarat Road, Musi, Pakchong, Nakhon Ratchasima 30130
TEL: *(01) 213 8435* **FAX:** *(01) 213 0785*
LOCATION: *On Route 2029, fork left after approximately 30km, then 9km to the course*
COURSE: *18 holes, 7102yd/6494m, par 72*
TYPE OF COURSE: *A testing desert-style layout winding through natural terrain with links characteristics*
DESIGNER: *Jack Nicklaus (1993)*
GREEN FEES: *BB*
FACILITIES: *Golf shop, caddies, cart and golf equipment hire, shoe and umbrella rental, driving range, putting green, changing facilities, swimming pool, refreshment shelters on course, coffee shop in clubhouse*
VISITORS: *Welcome, but advance reservation necessary; closed Monday*

This is another Jack Nicklaus design, which offers a refreshing contrast to the essentially manufactured holes at Mission Hills. Laid out across a relatively level valley floor surrounded by wooded hills, this course has a more natural, almost rustic, feel. Away from the fairways, the rough is fearsome; there is a premium on accuracy. Apart from the greens, the condition of the course is only moderately good. This state of affairs is clearly related to the club's past financial problems. However, in some respects, this has helped to create a more relaxed and pleasant atmosphere on the course, where the player can feel at one with nature. Many of the holes flow through a peaceful, untouched wilderness, which is rich with natural flora and wildlife.

On the front nine, the 543-yd/496-m 3rd is a great par 5. You drive over a water ditch to an uphill fairway with a large central tree. Your second has to find a small, narrow island of fairway edging a large water hazard left, which you then have to carry to reach the angled green. Coming home, the 386-yd/353-m 16th is a demanding dogleg right round a large lake, with sand on the corner. The green is on a sort of promontory in the water, and is well protected by sand. The safer you go left off the tee, the longer your approach.

Below: Relaxed golf in a very natural landscape backed by wooded hills.

4 *Friendship Meadows*

*Friendship Meadows Country Club, 20/1 Moo 16,
Mittraparb Road, Km 162, Pakchong, Nakhon
Ratchasima 30130*
TEL: *(044) 311 571, 313 245, 315 136* **FAX:**
(044) 312 955
LOCATION: *Near Muak-Lek; Km 162 marker on
Route 2*
COURSE: *18 holes, 6531yd/5972m, par 72*
TYPE OF COURSE: *Severely undulating parkland with
mature trees*
DESIGNER: *Nelson, Wright & Howarth (1995)*
GREEN FEES: *BB*
FACILITIES: *Golf shop, caddies, cart and golf equipment
hire, shoe and umbrella rental, driving range, putting
green, changing facilities, on-course refreshment shelters,
clubhouse restaurant*
VISITORS: *Welcome, but telephone in advance. Closed
Mondays*

If golf clubs can be said to have character,
then this one is as friendly as its name
implies. It is a relatively new, unpretentious
members' club where the visitor is made most
welcome. The course, although fairly short, is
full of interest because of the severely
undulating land on which it has been built.

This is very much a course fashioned by the
nature of the site.

There is a sprinkling of water hazards,
although few really affect play, and the
bunkering is not too penal. What really makes
this course interesting are the dramatic changes
of elevation, allied to a judicious retention of
certain large mature trees and strategic use of
the slopes, swales, humps and hollows existing
on the terrain. The surrounding scenery, with
views of densely wooded hills and distant
mountains, is peaceful and relaxing – the ideal
antidote to urban pressures.

One of the better holes is the 407–yd/
372–m 4th. This has a tee shot across water to
a tilted, bunkered fairway turning left past
impenetrable rough on the corner and uphill
to a blind, elevated, well-bunkered green.

The clubhouse is small but adequate.
Future plans include a further nine holes, a
hotel, tennis courts and a shopping centre.

*Below: Rolling slopes and superb hilltop views create an
extremely interesting course.*

Unusual Courses

Golf is a game that is infinitely capable of adaptation to circumstances. For example, the 36-hole inaugural British Open in 1860 was played over three circuits of the Prestwick links, then only 12 holes. Thailand, land of the regular six-ball, also has many examples of unusual courses. Two of the oldest courses, the Royal Bangkok Sports Club and the Royal Dusit Golf Club, were laid out within horse-racing circuits, at the time the only viable space available. Built on sacrosanct royal land around the turn of the 19th century, they remain the two most downtown city courses in the world.

Above: Golf within the race track at Royal Bangkok Sports Club, dwarfed by downtown highrises and the new Skytrain on the right.

Another unique layout is the Royal Thai Air Force golf course at Don Muang, Bangkok's international airport. A long sliver of green, just two narrow fairways wide, it has 18 holes squeezed between the two main runways. It was host to the Thailand Open between 1965 and 1972. The 27-hole course of Panya Indra, near Bangkok, has 18 holes that can be floodlit at night. The Bangkok Golf Club also has a unique nine-hole par 3 course, where each is a replica of a world-famous short hole, such as the 11th at St Andrews or the 12th at Augusta. Subhapruek Country Club at Bangbor has the last word – a full-size 19th hole par 3 over water that is a part of the main course.

Below: Holing out between the two runways on Kantarat golf course at Don Muang airport.

REGIONAL DIRECTORY

Where to Stay

Before the arrival of golf in 1992–3, demand for upmarket accommodation in an area dominated by craggy mountains, pastoral dairy and fruit farms and the large Khao Yai National Park was limited.

Saraburi

Forest Hills Country Club (036 341 911-4, Fax: 036 341 732) Occupying high ground with exceptional views out over the golf course and surrounding mountains, the Sir James Lodge is interconnected with the golf clubhouse, offering very comfortable accommodation and a good range of facilities. The 143 guest rooms and suites all have cable TV, mini bar and en-suite bathroom, while the adjoining clubhouse has both the comprehensive Putters coffee shop offering Thai and continental cuisine and Bayards grill room. Apart from golf, there is a large swimming pool, tennis courts, fitness centre, sauna, snooker room and library. Out on the rolling wooded estate, there are a variety of watersports, horse riding, a shooting range and nature trails.

Khao Yai Cowboy City Resort (044 297 471-9, Fax: 044 297 465) For something completely different, this faux western ranch is designed to appeal to weekend cowboys. It offers rustic bungalows behind a central 'saloon'. There is a Steak and Beer House, a swimming pool, an opal factory alongside, and opportunities for horseback riding with tuition. Ideal for kids of all ages.

Pakchong

Mission Hills Golf Club (044 297 261, 044 297 259) Planned as part of the best five-star resort in Thailand, the palatial clubhouse/hotel, a feast of marbled grandeur, has recently fallen on hard times. However, the course is first-class. In a dramatic location with scenic mountain views, bargain room rates will sweeten the pill of rather basic coffee-shop service. Other facilities include a free-form swimming pool, fitness room, sauna and steam, Jacuzzi and snooker. Go for the golf.

Where to Eat

Without transport you will find it hard to go anywhere to eat outside your hotel in this still undeveloped area. The town of Pakchong has a few streetside restaurants serving Thai and Chinese food. Nearby Muak-lek is cow country, and beef dominates the menu of the **Farmhouse Inn** and the Western-themed **Chokchai Steak House**.

What to See

The central feature of this region is the **Khao Yai National Park**, the oldest and third-largest in the country. It will reward anyone interested in discovering a wide variety of flora and fauna in its natural, untouched habitat. The range of species is quite remarkable (see p.82) and organized tours or renting your own car with driver will pay dividends. A little to the north-east is Nakhon Ratchasima and the gateway to the ancient temples of **Phimai** (see p.83). Local handicrafts in the region include the bronzed pottery of **Dan Kwian** and cotton phakit weaving from **Nong Khai,** and the treasured *matmi* silk from **Khon Kaen**.

Below: Par for the course – caddies assist with umbrella, chair and golf bag.

Chapter 4

Northern Region

If any region could be said to be purpose-built for tourism, it has to be the north. Occupying around a quarter of the country's land mass, this largely mountainous area, bordered by Myanmar and Laos, is rich in history, ethnic variety and culture. It has a noticeably cooler climate than the rest of Thailand and features the country's highest mountain, the picturesque and colourful people of the hill-tribes (see p.106), a large number of ancient temples, the Kingdom's oldest golf club, reputedly the country's most beautiful women, and a broad selection of handicrafts. The area has its own dialects, cuisine, music, costume and festivals.

While much of Thailand's early history evolved around the ancient cities of Sukhothai and later Ayutthaya, the north formed the separate kingdom of Lanna, which was founded by King Mengrai in the mid–13th century. He created its two main cities, Chiang Rai and later Chiang Mai. The latter is now the country's second largest city and was the seat of the independent Lanna kingdom for more than 200 years until it was overthrown by the Burmese. These influences can be found in all aspects of northern life, and they provide a truly fascinating contrast to the other regions.

The environs of the two main cities offer excellent golf, but every visitor should also 'smell the flowers along the way'. Chiang Mai, the Rose of the North, lies 700km/440 miles from Bangkok and displays fine examples of its historic past. You can see the square, water-filled moat that surrounded the original city and remnants of the defensive walls. Many ancient temples, dating back to the 13th

Left: The golden glory of Wat Phra That Doi Suthep, Chiang Mai. Above: Snacks and smiles at a refreshment stop on Santiburi golf course.

century, reflect the influence of Buddhism and the elegant craftsmanship for which the region is noted. Most famous is Wat Phra That Doi Suthep, overlooking the city more than 1067m/3500ft above sea level from the crest of a forested mountain. Dating from 1383, access at the top is either up a 290-step ceremonial staircase or via funicular. The golden pagoda attracts pilgrims from around the globe, as does the sensational view.

A two-and-a-half hour drive or a brief flight north-east from Chiang Mai brings you to the original capital of the Lanna Thai kingdom, Chiang Rai. This was founded in 1262. Here too, ancient city walls and ornate temples bear witness to a long history. This is the access point for visiting the colourful hilltribes in their native mountain habitats and to the Golden Triangle, long infamous as a world centre of opium production. Although drug cultivation has been replaced, this dramatic location of the meeting of three countries – Thailand, Myanmar and Laos – alongside the mighty Mekong River, is a popular tourist destination.

Other excursions are to the dramatic mountain edge of Phu Chee Fah, overlooking Laos, and Doi Tung. At just

SPIRIT HOUSES

Thai people believe all land was inhabited by spirits before humans moved in. When building a new house, a miniature replica of a traditional Thai house or temple is erected on a pedestal on the site to give the spirits a home of their own. Daily offerings of food, water and flower garlands, even an umbrella as cover from the rain, are made to please the spirits and bring good luck (back cover).

over 1500m/4922ft, this beautiful mountainside was formerly a major centre for opium production. Under the energetic patronage of the present King's late mother, it was converted into a magnificent floral garden, where the cooler conditions encourage many varieties. This is also a notable location for many handicrafts and cottage industries, including handmade carpets and paper items made from the bark of mulberry trees.

The northern region provides excellent opportunities for purchasing samples of attractive local handicrafts, particularly around Chiang Mai. Along the Bo San Kamphaeng Road, one can watch the production of many items, including hand-painted parasols in silk or mulberry paper, folding fans of all sizes, woven cotton and silk, silver and lacquerware, wood carving, celadon pottery and basketry.

Local cuisine tends to be less spicy than in the south and also reflects Burmese and Chinese influences. Various varieties of local sausage are popular, as is a dish featuring sticky rice with fresh mango, topped off with coconut milk and nuts. A *khantoke* dinner is typical, with a variety of small bowls shared between diners sitting round a small raised table.

ROYAL JUMBOS

Since early times, elephants have played a major role in Thailand's culture and economy. Royalty and nobility led their armies into battle on them. They were used as mounts for hunting and, with their size and strength, played an important role in teak logging. Many still live in the wild, while a rare white elephant, if found, is considered auspicious and presented to the king. An elephant used to appear on the national flag and an annual elephant event is held at Surin in the north-east.

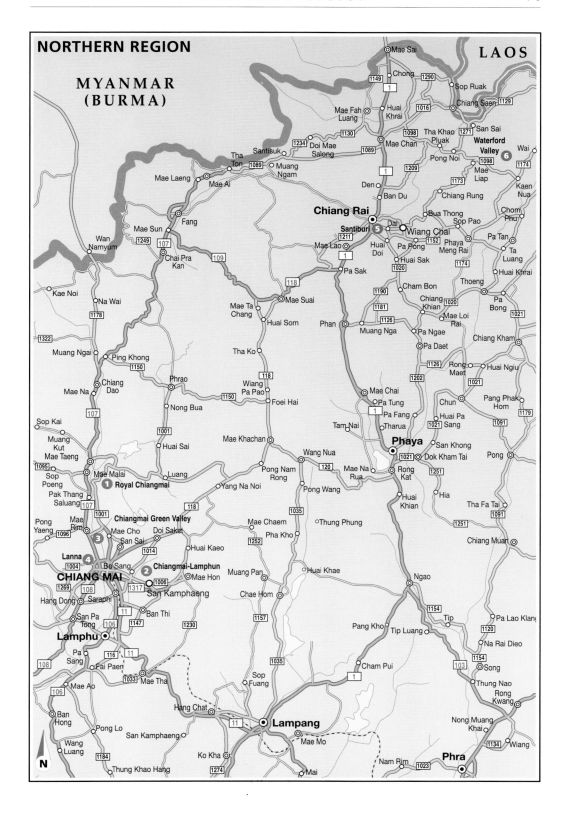

NORTHERN REGION

MYANMAR (BURMA)

LAOS

Royal Chiangmai

*The Royal Chiangmai Golf Resort, 169 Moo 5,
Chiangmai–Prao Road, T.Maefak, A.Sansai,
Chiang Mai 50290*
TEL: *(053) 849 301-6* **FAX:** *(053) 849 310*
EMAIL: *golf1@cm.ksc.co.th, ctiden@cm.ksc.co.th*
LOCATION: *Km 26 Chiangmai-Prao Road, Route
1001*
COURSE: *18 holes, 6969yd/6372m, par 72*
TYPE OF COURSE: *Parkland with some links character*
DESIGNER: *Peter W. Thomson (1996)*
GREEN FEES: *BB*
FACILITIES: *Golf shop, caddies, cart and equipment
hire, shoe and chair and umbrella rental, driving range,
putting green, 18-hole putting course, changing facilities,
refreshment shelters on course, restaurant in clubhouse,
adjacent hotel with swimming pool, sauna and gym,
snooker, karaoke, Thai massage*
VISITORS: *Welcome, but an advance telephone call is
advised*

ROYAL CHIANGMAI

HOLE	YD	M	PAR	HOLE	YD	M	PAR
1	396	362	4	10	397	363	4
2	361	330	4	11	172	157	3
3	160	146	3	12	565	517	5
4	438	400	4	13	409	374	4
5	563	515	5	14	374	342	4
6	202	185	3	15	584	534	5
7	358	327	4	16	418	382	4
8	543	496	5	17	173	158	3
9	428	391	4	18	428	391	4
OUT	3449	3154	36	IN	3520	3219	36

6969YD • 6372M • PAR 72

Too many new courses are built to a
championship specification. These are
designed to test the best players, but, in the
process, end up humbling the majority who
only want to play for pleasure. Luckily, Royal
Chiangmai, roughly 30 minutes' drive north
of Chiang Mai city, is a genuine resort course.
Golfing legend Peter W. Thomson has taken
a fairly compact, gently sloping site and
produced some extremely enjoyable golf for
players of all levels. Ringed by a series of
tree-encrusted hills backed by distant
mountains and maintained in
immaculate condition, the
course is one of
those rare treats
that keeps you
wanting to
come back

and play more. This is essentially a course to
enjoy, whatever your score, but since it tends
to play somewhat shorter than the card, you
may have a pleasant surprise.

Each hole presents a different examination
and a different delight. Well-placed trees add
definition, as do the very visible bunkers.
There is plenty of movement, a lot of subtle
undulation in the fairways, producing a
number of sloping lies very much in the style
of seaside links golf. The elevated greens are
protected by sand, but only relatively little
strategic water, and have interesting
but always fair slopes. There are
many flowering trees,

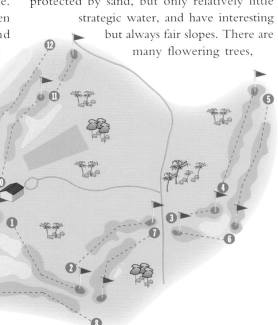

little waterfalls, tall palms, colourful shrubs, mangos, bananas, coconuts and lychees. All fit in naturally – there is none of the artificiality prevalent in some Thai courses.

The 2nd hole typifies the natural 'links' feel. Not long, it requires finesse off the tee to avoid an obstructive tree and sand on the corner of the right-hand dogleg, plus an accurate approach from the rippling fairway to hold the multilevel green. The 7th is another attractive challenge, curving left round water with a nest of three Scottish-style bunkers dead ahead and a smallish, elevated green. The par 5 15th has class (see p.21), while the short, very floral 17th requires a high carry over water and four bunkers to hold an elevated, angled target.

This is a genuinely delightful resort location, compact and well organized with many facilities, yet not too far from the

Above: The 17th presents a small elevated green across water. Below: The approach to the uphill 9th with the elegant raised clubhouse behind.

attractions of the city. The on-site hotel has 52 rooms and four suites, all with fine views out over the course and surrounding hills, one of which shelters an attractive Thai temple. Guests can enjoy a fitness room, snooker and karaoke. Between the hotel building and the golf course there is an attractive swimming pool and a full 18-hole putting course, complete with hazards.

Royal Chiangmai lives up to its name – it is a royal treat to play, offering natural, seaside links-style golf in a wholly tropical setting.

Chiangmai-Lamphun

Chiangmai-Lamphun Golf Club, San Kamphaeng-Banthi, Chiang Mai 50130
TEL: *(053) 880 880-4* **FAX:** *(053) 880 888, 201 607*
WWW: *www.chiangmaigolf.com*
LOCATION: *20km east of Chiang Mai city on Route 1006*
COURSE: *18 holes, 6919yd/6327m, par 72*
TYPE OF COURSE: *Parkland along a well-wooded river valley*
DESIGNER: *Dr Sukhum Sukapanpotharam (1990)*
GREEN FEES: *BBB*
FACILITIES: *Golf shop, caddies, cart and golf equipment hire, shoe and umbrella rental, driving range, putting green, changing facilities, snack shelters on course, restaurant in clubhouse*
VISITORS: *Visitors welcome, but advance reservation requested. Soft spike rule planned*

CHIANGMAI-LAMPHUN

HOLE	YD	M	PAR	HOLE	YD	M	PAR
1	511	467	5	10	373	341	4
2	408	373	4	11	215	196	3
3	203	185	3	12	377	345	4
4	552	505	5	13	590	539	5
5	166	152	3	14	407	372	4
6	384	351	4	15	177	162	3
7	373	341	4	16	393	359	4
8	398	364	4	17	422	386	4
9	421	385	4	18	549	502	5
OUT	3416	3123	36	IN	3503	3203	36

6919YD • 6327M • PAR 72

This is a most interesting, well-established golf course in an idyllic setting. It is laid out along a winding creek in a valley flanked by hills cloaked in a verdant cascade of evergreen. It is a superb place to play, not too far from town, with a wealth of attractive, mature flowering trees and shrubs. Few places can engender such feelings of peaceful isolation, of being far from anywhere. The background chirping of crickets linked in with a blaze of butterflies makes an extremely pleasant setting for golf.

The course, following the slopes of a natural creek past many ancient trees, demands precision and placement off the tee, often to avoid lone fairway trees affecting the line of play. Gentle mounding,

shallow bunkers and the movement of the land itself, all help to create a most natural feeling. The course was conceived and designed by a local golf enthusiast, Dr Sukhum. It is a most successful first effort by someone who, although not a professional golf architect, had an intuitive understanding of what was required, combined with a love of the game and an open mind. Also – in common with many well-respected courses created in Scotland a century ago – deciding to leave well alone where nature had already made the ideal land for golf has proven successful. Dr Sukhum's comments on his course are revealing. 'I moved from Bangkok to found a faculty of engineering at Chiang Mai University and played golf both at the Gymkhana and Lanna 9-hole courses. I

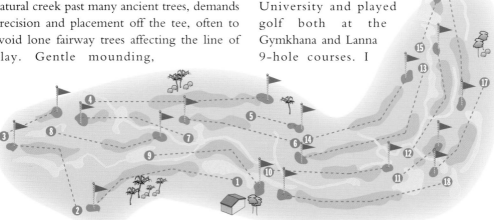

Above: Nestling in a secluded valley, the course winds past attractive flowering shrubs and trees.

was a member of the latter, a military course, and was teeing off with some friends, when we had to stand aside to let a general play first. We felt this attitude was not how golf should be played among members and we discussed the possibility of building a new course. About ten years later, we formed a company between friends and relatives. Finding the right site, with sufficient land in such a beautiful setting, was difficult. I bought the land, designed the course, built it and now operate it. I had no previous experience; I studied other courses, including the Masters on television, but have not tried to copy anything. I studied nature, keeping as many existing trees as possible. I hope the course looks long-established, perhaps for 50 years or more, rather than only since 1990. Leaving trees within the fairway, as at the 9th and the 18th, works on the mind, making holes look narrower than they actually play. One should also never forget that while using nature as a sporting place, you should respect it and the culture of the game. I wanted people to enjoy playing the course but also that it could test the best, as has been proven in a number of pro and amateur events played here, including the 1995 South East Asian Games. It is not long, just a few yards more than Augusta, but highly strategic with much variety.'

FLORAL FANTASY

Thai flower arrangement is a complex art form. Originally a pastime of ladies of the royal court, the intricate hanging garlands and complex decorations for presentation are more akin to floral jewellery. The most common is the *malai*, made from fragrant white jasmine buds threaded with roses, marigolds or orchids. Other arrangements include elegant *krathongs* (see p.111) and *poom*, a budding lotus shape tightly embedded with flowers.

Chiangmai Green Valley

*Chiangmai Green Valley Country Club, 183/2 Moo
1, Chotana Road, (Chiangmai-Maerim), Mae-Sa,
Mae Rim, Chiang Mai 50180*
TEL: *(053) 298 249-51, 298 220-3* **FAX:** *(053)
297 426*
EMAIL: *gvalley@asianet.co.th*
LOCATION: *18km north of Chiang Mai airport,
Route 107*
COURSE: *18 holes, 7205yd/6588m, par 72*
TYPE OF COURSE: *Modern international design with
much sand and water*
DESIGNER: *Dennis Griffiths (1990)*
GREEN FEES: *BB*
FACILITIES: *Pro shop, caddies, cart and golf equipment
hire, shoe and umbrella rental, driving range, putting
green, changing facilities, sauna and steam bath, snack
shelters on course, bar and restaurants in large clubhouse*
VISITORS: *Visitors welcome, but advance booking
necessary. Soft spikes required; closed Tuesday*

Laid out over an area of level land with
distant mountain views, this is a prime
example of a modern course constructed to
international standards. It is raised well above
the ever-present water in a series of palm-
speckled green peninsulas and islands. It is
kept 90 per cent chemical-free and thus eco-
friendly. There are many birds, lizards and
other wildlife, but an absence of colourful
flowers. This greenkeeping policy tends to
create slightly tired-looking, weedy holes that
are very playable nonetheless. Each fairway is
lined with large palms and many track above
slopes leading down to penal water. Some of
the fairways are built in two levels; most have
flat-floored, mounded bunkers to the sides,
which are, to an extent, out of sight. There
are a number of very large areas of strategic
sand, much around some elevated greens and
a series of water carries, in two cases to
elevated, island greens. This is reckoned to be
the busiest course in the Chiang Mai area,
where drinks shelters every three holes display
plans of the next three, with the aim to
improve strategy and speed up play.

*Below: Clubhouse view out over the course, with its many
lakes, palm trees and views of Doi Suthep mountain rising
in the background.*

Lanna Sports Centre

Lanna Sports Centre, Chotana Road, Muang, Chiang Mai 50300

TEL: *(053) 221 911* **FAX:** *(053) 221 743*
EMAIL: *kcalfee@loxinfo.co.th*
LOCATION: *2km north of the Chiang Mai ring road on Route 107*
COURSE: *27 holes – Course 1 and 2 7174yd/6560m; 1 and 3 6887yd/6297m; 2 and 3 6865yd/6277m; all par 72*
TYPE OF COURSE: *Mature parkland with mountain views*
DESIGNER: *Col Chana Chayakul (1974, 1975); Dr Sukitti Klangvisai (1993)*
GREEN FEES: *BB*
FACILITIES: *Golf shop, caddies, cart and golf equipment hire, shoe and umbrella rental, two-tier driving range, contoured chipping and putting green, changing facilities, drink shelters on course, restaurant in Thai-style clubhouse, basketball, badminton, snooker, Olympic-size swimming pool, tennis, gun club, horse riding and sauna/fitness rooms*
VISITORS: *Visitors welcome, but advance telephone call advised*

There is a timeless air about this golf and sports complex, even though the first nine holes (Course 1) date from only 1974.

This was originally a fairly rustic facility, primarily for military use. Still managed by the Royal Thai Army, the course has been expanded to three interchangeable nines. The most recent of these (Course 3), is of attractive, modern landscaped design. It is laid out on land within an adjacent horse-racing circuit.

The setting is majestic. There are large, mature trees, some left within the fairway, backed by the historic Doi Suthep mountain and its famous temple. The well-elevated tees, greens and hazards of the original 18 reflect another era, but the often sloping surfaces putt well and the holes play their full length. The newest nine is in complete contrast. It has undulating fairways, mounded, well-shaped greens and colourful shrubs and flowers bordering highly strategic lakes. The course is in a very pleasant situation close to town, and offers a wealth of other sporting facilities.

Below: The newest nine holes at Lanna hark back to another era, being mainly laid out within the confines of the horse-racing circuit.

Santiburi Country Club

*Santiburi Country Club, 12 Moo 3, Sai Huaidoi–Sop
Pao Road, Wiangchai Province, Chiang Rai 57210*
TEL: *(053) 662 821-6* **FAX:** *(053) 717 377*
LOCATION: *8km south-east of Chiang Rai on Route
1152*
COURSE: *18 holes 6981yd/6383m, par 72*
TYPE OF COURSE: *Undulating parkland backed by
mountains*
DESIGNER: *Robert Trent Jones Jr (1992)*
GREEN FEES: *BBB*
FACILITIES: *Golf shop, caddies, cart and equipment
hire, chair rental, driving range, pitching and putting
greens, changing facilities, sauna, refreshment shelters on
course, catering in clubhouse*
VISITORS: *Welcome, but an advance telephone call is
suggested. Soft spikes only*

SANTIBURI

HOLE	YD	M	PAR	HOLE	YD	M	PAR
1	525	480	5	10	400	366	4
2	414	378	4	11	357	326	4
3	218	199	3	12	147	134	3
4	364	333	4	13	516	472	5
5	418	382	4	14	402	367	4
6	582	532	5	15	427	390	4
7	196	179	3	16	462	422	4
8	386	353	4	17	160	146	3
9	441	403	4	18	566	517	5
OUT	3544	3241	36	IN	3437	3143	36

6981YD • 6383M • PAR 72

Any listing of the best courses in Thailand inevitably puts Santiburi near the top and with good reason. Tucked away close to the northern city of Chiang Rai, this very understated semi-private members' club offers superbly conditioned golf in a most attractive location. Only a few minutes' drive from town, it offers a sense of tranquillity and harmony with nature, with its lakes and rolling slopes reflecting the calm of the surrounding mountains.

The course is another example of the talent of American architect Robert Trent Jones Jr, also evident at Navatanee, President and Eastern Star. Over the gently rolling wooded hills and slopes of the property, he has fashioned a course that can provide endless pleasure for members from the tees of the day, while still requiring them to play well to score, but which also offers a test for the professionals from the back markers.

The fairways and greens are elegantly manicured but, with the lush Bermuda grass, there is hardly any run on the ball and the

holes play their full length. There is little formal gardening, rather the joy of seemingly haphazard banks of wild flowers and sweet-scented flowering trees.

Santiburi has been planned as a very exclusive golf club and residential community, with all the essential, if low-key, facilities that such an operation requires. The fine timbered northern-style clubhouse is set on a hilltop. It offers a magnificent panorama out over the property from the upper terrace, which also offers informal dining and superb sunset views. The locker rooms are elegant and there is the refreshing welcome of a cologne-sprinkled cold towel and a glass of iced water when you return from the course.

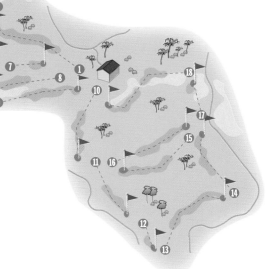

Above: Driving off at the 10th, an uphill curving dogleg left, with wonderful mountain views. Below: The large practice putting green with the 1st hole winding away through the trees beyond.

Another treat is the experienced service offered by the caddies in their dusky pink uniforms. It's a good idea to take their advice, since the sloping greens have many subtle lines. Although originally sown with Tifdwarf, the fifth green has recently been changed to the latest development, TifEagle, presaging the likely eventual conversion of the entire 18.

The course divides itself into two distinct halves. The front nine, with a series of gently undulating holes, has water affecting play on seven of them, most notably at the 4th and 8th. Neither are particularly long, but each demands an approach threatened by a semi-hidden lake eating in front of the shallow, steeply sloping green. The back nine, in complete contrast, flows and turns over and around a series of wooded hills, with strategic

water only apparent on the closing two. The 17th, played across a pond to a shallow, angled green, bunkered back and front, is a deceptive distance. It also offers a series of subtle slopes in the green itself. The double-dogleg 18th is a great finishing hole (see p.21).

Although not easy to score on, with lush Bermuda rough, deceptive distances and a number of challenging water hazards, Santiburi is a definite treat to play, a real pleasure and certainly demands a visit.

Waterford Valley

Waterford Valley Golf Club, 333 Moo 5, Tambon Pasang, Wiang Chai, Chiang Rai 57210
TEL: *(053) 953 425-7, 953 445* **FAX:** *(053) 953 447*
LOCATION: *Wiangchai Hills, approx. 23km northeast of Chiang Rai city, Route 1173*
COURSE: *18 holes, 6961yd/6365m, par 72*
TYPE OF COURSE: *Modern parkland on and around two hills*
DESIGNER *Rathert International Golf Design (1996)*
GREEN FEES: *BB*
FACILITIES: *Golf shop, caddies, cart and golf equipment hire, driving range, putting green, changing facilities, snack shelters on course, restaurant in clubhouse, all-suite golf lodge on site overlooking the golf course, swimming pool*
VISITORS: *Visitors welcome, but an advance telephone call appreciated*

HOLE	YD	M	PAR	HOLE	YD	M	PAR
1	505	462	5	10	382	349	4
2	168	154	3	11	535	489	5
3	478	437	4	12	185	169	3
4	364	333	4	13	415	379	4
5	439	401	4	14	444	406	4
6	226	207	3	15	197	180	3
7	406	371	4	16	367	335	4
8	559	511	5	17	533	487	5
9	368	336	4	18	390	357	4
OUT	3513	3212	36	IN	3448	3153	36

WATERFORD VALLEY

6961YD •6365M • PAR 72

L ike Rome, the infrastructure of this resort course is located on the summits of a series of hills, with the golf course falling away to the valley floor below. Waterford Valley is about 45 minutes from Chiang Rai city, but a new highway should reduce this to half-an-hour. It is worth the trip, since this delightfully rural location offers fine views from the higher ground across a broad valley to the pastel shades of distant mountains. There is also extremely pleasant hilltop mini-suite accommodation on site. This is decorated in simple, Japanese-style décor in pale wood and tiles, with a large round bath plus a shower, and a sitting room leading out to individual balcony views over the course. The club offers a number of attractive inclusive golf packages, should you make the decision to stay.

Still relatively new, the golf course is improving all the time. With the natural slope of the hillsides coming into play on roughly half the holes, it presents a very interesting challenge. Although the gradient on the fairways is always perfectly fair and a long way from being in the category of mountain golf, you may find negotiating the hills quite tough in the heat and a golf cart (with attendant caddies) is recommended. Apart from the good use of the sloping land (which is what makes the golf course so full of interest), the design is a little bland and uninspired. The fairways are broad, the bunkers shallow and the attractive water hazards, although penal, should only catch the thoughtless or the inveterate slicer.

The course, however, is kept in good condition with firm, fast, and often elevated greens, some of which offer very testing lines. It offers exactly the right combination of golfing challenge and delightful views to attract the holiday golfer. A further feature are the flowering shrubs, trees and colourful floral displays, which greet the player at every turn.

From the clubhouse terrace, open to any cooling breeze, there are superb views down the 505-yd/462-m par 5 first hole (1A). This has its tee-shot played out over a suspended lake to a fairway plateau. The longer hitter may be tempted to try for two on, but the further fairway offers difficult downhill lies and the narrow green is angled to the approach. Terrace viewers can also follow play approaching up the sharp dogleg uphill 9th of the B course (390yd/357m). The second shot is over the same lake and up to a steeply sloping, well-bunkered green. Here is an excellent example of a hole where you will need more club than you think. Overall, the

course presents a very fair examination, with all the hazards visible and no blind uphill shots, despite the slopes.

With the colourful varieties of floral display, the very natural landscape bordering the holes and lakes, plus the supporting backdrop of the surrounding Wiangchai Hills, this is a most pleasant golfing location. It offers a nice contrast to some of the rather level courses in other regions.

Above: Side view of the downhill 1st hole (A). Below: The clubhouse aspect of 9th green (B), looking back up the fairway to distant hills.

Hilltribe People

The hilltribes, (more correctly termed mountain people) of northern Thailand form a colourful selection of highly distinctive ethnic groups. Most are settled in the mountainous north, having migrated (often many centuries ago) from Mongolia, China, Tibet and Myanmar. They still retain their independence, their unique and vibrant costumes, and their own languages, customs and culture. They are semi-nomadic and survive from indiscriminate farming (which at one time included the notorious opium poppy) and various forms of handicrafts, which make popular purchases with foreign visitors.

There are six major tribes, which number 500,000 out of Thailand's population of more than 60 million. They are

A Yao lady wearing and working on samples of their renowned embroidery.

mainly located, at various altitudes, in the northern regions of Chiang Rai, Phayao, Chiang Mai and Mae Hong Son. They live in closely integrated mountain village communities where they pursue a way of life comparatively untouched by lowland development. This includes a spirituality based on various forms of animism and ancient beliefs about the existence of spirits and the encouragement of good fortune. Their houses are simple wooden structures, often raised on stilts, with *atap* grass roofs. These normally house the extended family.

The largest group is the Karen, comprising more than half of the total of the mountain people. Originally from Myanmar, they are noted for agriculture, weaving and providing the best *mahouts* (elephant handlers). They also have a distinctive sub-group, the Padaung, whose 'long neck' females wear tight collars of numerous brass rings, the number increasing with the woman's age.

Tourists who visit the bustling night bazaars in the main towns looking for souvenirs, or go to local markets for fruit and vegetables, are likely to encounter the Akha and Yao tribeswomen. The former wear costumes based on a black jacket, skirt and leggings that are beautifully embroidered in colourful stripes, topped with an ornate red-and-white headdress laden with silver balls and coins. Yao costume is more reserved, the black jacket having thick red woollen lapels (see photo) and much embroidery, as does the black turban. The embroidered items that are among the many handicrafts they offer for sale are exquisitely made and highly prized.

Other hilltribes include the Hmong, originally from western China; the Lisu, from eastern Tibet; and the Lahu, from south-west China via Myanmar. Each has a distinctive way of life that can be observed by visiting their remote mountain villages through a number of specialized day tours. They are open and friendly with visitors and deserve to be treated with appropriate courtesy and respect, representing as they do cultures and lifestyles that have remained unchanged for centuries.

REGIONAL DIRECTORY

Where to Stay
Chiang Mai

Royal Princess (053 281 033-43, Fax: 053 281 044) Located in the heart of Thailand's second-largest city, by the famous Night Bazaar, this well-appointed hotel is part of the Dusit Group. It is ideally situated for shopping and sightseeing. There are 200 comfortably furnished rooms and suites, and a choice of dining in the Jasmine Chinese and Miyuki Japanese restaurants, as well as a full range of Thai and international fare in the Coffee Shop. Facilities include a lobby bar, night club, secluded swimming pool and Yogi traditional Thai massage.

Chiang Mai Plaza Hotel (053 270 036-50, Fax: 053 279 457) Despite its size (there are 440 guest rooms and suites), this centrally located hotel conveys a warm welcome typical of the 'Rose of the North'. It combines efficiency with elegant décor based on the fabled Lanna era. Although favoured for business meetings and conventions, individuals are also very welome. The Faikum restaurant serves both international and Thai food, with a popular dim sum lunch. The swimming pool serves light meals and snacks; there is also a fitness centre and snooker club.

Where to Eat
The range of dining out in this popular destination means that there should be something to satisfy all tastes. There are Thai, Chinese, Vietnamese, Japanese, Indian, Arab, Italian, French, Swiss, German, Swedish, Mexican, and even British restaurants, as well as a number of pubs and Western-style delis. For something special, visit **Le Coq d'Or** (053 282 024) for elegant dining and fine wines in a tasteful mansion (formerly the US Embassy). They even collect you from your hotel in an old black London cab! Italian food with flair awaits at **Piccola Roma Palace** (053 820 297). For something a little different, try **River Cruise Seafood** (053 274 822) with lunch or dinner on the Mae Ping River.

What to See
The **Doi Inthanon National Park** has waterfalls, flowers, exotic birds and much more. Two famous handicraft villages deserve a visit – **Bo Sang** for hand-painted silk, cotton and mulberry paper umbrellas and fans; **San Kamphaeng** for superb hand-woven silks and cottons. **Doi Suthep** (see p.92) offers a majestic temple with a view. Elephant shows and jungle rides as well as river rafting can be enjoyed at **Mae Sa** or **Taeng Dao** elephant camps.

Where to Stay
Chiang Rai

Dusit Island Resort (053 715 777-9, Fax: 053 715 801) Set on its own island in the Kok River just outside the town with spectacular mountains behind, this deluxe hotel offers a comfortable base from which to visit the Night Bazaar, play golf or explore the region. The 271 guest rooms and suites have river views and exceptional levels of service. In addition to the Thai and international menu in the Island Cafe, The Peak steak house and Chinatown are two specialist restaurants, the former on the top floor with superb views. As an alternative, the Larn Tong Thai Pavilion provides Lanna-style *khantoke* dinners with traditional dancing in a garden setting. Facilities include swimming pool, fitness centre, tennis, Jacuzzi and steam rooms, Thai massage, snooker and a pub.

Wiang Inn Hotel (053 711 533, Fax: 053 711 877) Located right in the centre of town, a few minutes stroll from the Night Bazaar, this friendly hotel has much to offer. The 260 rooms and suites have traditional features, as does the popular coffee shop, which serves a good value lunchtime buffet. There is a lobby piano bar, swimming pool, Torino karaoke club and Orchid massage parlour.

Where to Eat
With a number of good hotels, there are many opportunities to sample both Western and Asian restaurant cuisine. Alternatively, there are numerous small establishments serving excellent Thai and Chinese food. Another good choice is the **Sa BanNga** restaurant, where typical northern *khantoke* dinners are accompanied by traditional music and dancing.

What to See
The northern location of Chiang Rai allows observation of its multicultural heritage at first-hand. Hilltribes (see p.106) are high on any list, with a visit to the mountain villages near the summit of **Doi Maesalong**. Nearby is **Doi Thung**, under Royal patronage, with beautiful gardens, mountain views and hilltribe handicrafts. Take a tour to the **Golden Triangle**, where the Mekong River (which links Tibet to the South China Sea) separates Myanmar, Laos and Thailand. A further town of interest on the Mekong is **Chiang Saen**, noted for its historic ancient ruins. Enjoy a spectacular view into Laos from the sheer grandeur of **Phu Chi Fa** mountain or the nine cascades of the **Pu Kaeng** waterfall in **Doi Luang National Park**. Near Mae Chan, the **Laan Tong Village** offers daily ethnic and dancing displays plus elephant rides.

Chapter 5

Western Kanchanaburi

This region, with its provincial capital of Kanchanaburi situated some two hours' drive north-west of Bangkok, is Thailand's third largest. It is a rugged area of great natural beauty stretching up to the border with Myanmar, where scenic mountains overlook winding river valleys and jungle forest. Unspoiled and still largely undeveloped, it has become a destination for tourists interested in exploring caves and dramatic waterfalls, and experiencing the drama and excitement of fast river rafting and canoeing, elephant trekking, lake fishing and other nature-based activities. Due to the area's relative proximity to Bangkok, attempts have been made to develop the area around Kanchanaburi town as a golfing resort destination. Its situation at the point where the Kwai Yai and Kwai Noi rivers meet to form the Mae Klong River and the consequent river valley locations have offered some attractive opportunities for development, with mixed results. Further to the south – around Ratchaburi – is another matter, with Dragon Hills arguably one the best resort courses in the country.

Leaving Bangkok and travelling west, one eventually comes to Nakhon Pathom, capital of a Mon kingdom from the 6th century to the 11th century. Without doubt, its main feature of cultural significance is known as the Pra Pathom Chedi. This is a huge inverted bell of glazed golden tiles, which, at 120m/393ft, is the tallest Buddhist monument in the world. Towards Kanchanaburi is Damnoen Saduak, where a daily floating market, that is now as much a tourist attraction as a market (arrive early), recalls an age of rural canals and water-borne transport.

Left: Water-borne traffic jams at the Damnoen Saduak floating market. Above: The restored wartime railway bridge over the River Kwai.

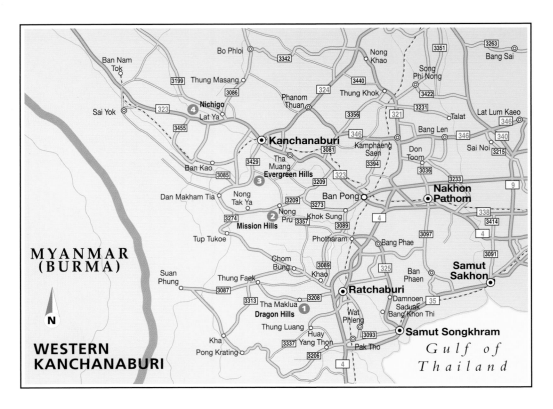

The largely unremarkable town of Kanchanaburi is primarily known for being on the route of the infamous railway that the Japanese constructed to connect Thailand with Myanmar during World War II. This was built at enormous cost in lives and suffering to the Allied prisoners of war and civilian labourers used in its construction. The famous railway bridge, rebuilt after destruction by Allied bombs, crosses the river at this location.

Kanchanaburi is the location for two museums dedicated to this tragic event and two official cemeteries, which contain the remains of more than 8700 men. The inhospitable nature of the surrounding terrain bears witness to the appalling difficulties encountered in the building of the railway by hand labour. This is particularly true of Hell Fire Pass, a deep rock-cutting 66km/41 miles to the north.

Above: Celebrating the Loy Krathong festival.
Left: Part of the main war cemetery, Kanchanaburi.

RAILWAY OF SHAME

No visitor to Kanchanaburi should ever forget the hardship suffered there during World War II. In 1942 the Japanese occupiers forced Allied prisoners of war and Asian civilians to construct a 415-km/258-mile railway line to connect Thanbyuzayat in Myanmar with Nong Pladuk in Thailand to ensure Japanese war supplies a safer route than the sea. Despite having only hand tools, insufficient food and sleep, appalling living conditions, no medical supplies, difficult jungle terrain and torrential monsoon rain, the forced labourers completed the project in 12 months. The cost, among such a malnourished, overworked and diseased labour force, was appalling – 13,000 Allied prisoners of war and 70,000 Asian conscripts died. The railway remains a testimony to the inhumanity of which man is capable.

Dragon Hills

Dragon Hills Golf and Country Club, 192 Moo 2,
Ang-Hin, Amphoe Paktor, Ratchaburi 70140
TEL: *(032) 261 205-7* **FAX:** *(032) 261 205*
LOCATION: *Route 3028 via Route 3337 and Route 4*
COURSE: *18 holes, 6812yd/6229m, par 72*
TYPE OF COURSE: *Heavily sculptured rural parkland*
DESIGNER: *Jim Engh (1994)*
GREEN FEES: *B*
FACILITIES: *Golf shop, caddies, cart and equipment*
hire, shoe and umbrella rental, driving range, pitching
and putting greens, changing facilities, refreshment
shelters on course, restaurant in clubhouse, on-site hotel
and bungalows
VISITORS: *Welcome, but advance telephone call advised*

DRAGON HILLS

HOLE	YD	M	PAR	HOLE	YD	M	PAR
1	376	344	4	10	428	391	4
2	377	345	4	11	520	475	5
3	182	166	3	12	181	165	3
4	564	516	5	13	531	485	5
5	386	353	4	14	197	180	3
6	172	157	3	15	572	523	5
7	405	370	4	16	390	357	4
8	523	478	5	17	193	176	3
9	381	348	4	18	434	397	4
OUT	3366	3078	36	IN	3446	3151	36

6812YD ¥ 6229M ¥ PAR 72

Thailand has many attractive golf courses, but few in a more outstanding location than this. A little less than two hours' drive west from Bangkok, the course is part of a 2300-acre estate in the Valley of the Dragon, nudging back into the foothills of the massive Bilauktaung mountain range, which forms a natural barrier with Myanmar. The rolling course runs in two loops around a hill and is named Dragon Pearl. It is the first of a p l a n n e d g o l f i n g trilogy, to i n c l u d e layouts by Jack Nicklaus and Isao Aoki as well as a golfing academy.

Dragon Hill's designer, American Jim Engh, while committed to major earth-moving, favours rounded rather than angular lines. He has cleverly managed to establish the course within the natural surroundings. Some holes have huge mounds, forming an amphitheatre round greens, echoing the mountain range looming behind. Others have grassy swales, pot bunkers, large expanses of sand and areas of natural rough leading to vast greens with sweeping slopes. These are often easy to reach, but even easier to three-putt.

You can have a great golf course and you can make sure that you keep it in exceptional condition, but you are very lucky if it is in a fabulous setting as well. Dragon Hills combines all three assets. The course is set amongst the beauty of natural, unspoiled countryside and cooled by breezes off the Andaman Sea. Its fairways wind and undulate past rivers with overhanging trees, scarlet flamboyants, placid lakes and quaint stone bridges. The layout itself is not overlong, but the rolling terrain and severe penalties for poor shotmaking make it a genuine test. Each hole is separate, and each is a delightful visual surprise, a procession of genuine interest and variety in a very peaceful, exclusive location.

All the short holes are memorable and characterize the designer's style. The 3rd is a carry over water and a large waste bunker to a long doglegged, two-level green turning left uphill backed by huge mounds – a great hole. The 6th is played across a depression of rough grasses to an uphill green surrounded with St Andrews-style pot bunkers. The 12th plays across a lake to a steeply sloped, three-level green, angled right towards the water. Finally, the 17th is a majestic hole, played downhill across rough country and a creek to a green part hidden behind a large hill right. Of the

Above: The approach to the par 5 11th, where a tough water carry and large waste bunker protect the green.
Below: The sweeping, undulating fairway of the par 5 13th, backed by thickly wooded hills.

longer holes, the 7th, seemingly innocuous, is a demanding par 4 (see p.19), while the 9th, after a broad welcoming fairway, turns sharply left to snake narrowly past mounds and sand to a small, semi-blind green.

The club offers golf with accommodation packages in either a secluded cluster of bungalows or a new, fairly functional, 50-room hotel on site. Only a handful of courses in Thailand are laid out in such a dramatic setting; few can match the quality of the golf.

Mission Hills

Mission Hills Golf Club, 27/7 Moo 7, Thambol Pang-Thru, Amphur Thamuang, Kanchanaburi 71110
TEL: *(034) 644 147-8* **FAX:** *(034) 644 147-8*
LOCATION: *Route 4 to Route 323, at Tha Ma Ka, take Route 3209 for the course*
COURSE: *18 holes, 7042yd/6439m, par 72*
TYPE OF COURSE: *Tropical parkland*
DESIGNER: *Jack Nicklaus (1991)*
GREEN FEES: *BB*
FACILITIES: *Golf shop, caddies, cart and equipment rental, umbrella hire, driving range, putting green, changing facilities, refreshment shelters on course, restaurant in clubhouse/resort hotel, swimming pool, sauna, exercise room, tennis, mountain bike and various watersports*
VISITORS: *Advance reservation necessary*

MISSION HILLS

HOLE	YD	M	PAR	HOLE	YD	M	PAR
1	513	469	5	10	444	406	4
2	379	346	4	11	163	149	3
3	175	160	3	12	545	498	5
4	430	393	4	13	399	365	4
5	440	402	4	14	417	381	4
6	219	200	3	15	409	374	4
7	410	375	4	16	189	173	3
8	553	505	5	17	361	330	4
9	452	413	4	18	548	501	5
OUT	3571	3265	36	IN	3475	3177	36

7042YD ¥ 6439M ¥ PAR 72

Near the small town of Kanchanaburi and less than two hours west of Bangkok, the golf resort of Mission Hills was the first to bear the Jack Nicklaus signature in Thailand. Followed shortly after by a second Mission Hills resort in Khao Yai, under the same ownership, there are now five Jack Nicklaus courses in the Kingdom, making him the most prolific overseas designer.

One of the advantages of visiting a course bearing the design

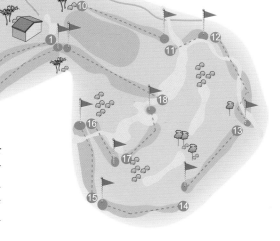

label of the mighty 'Golden Bear', wherever in the world you may be, is that you know what to expect. There will be no hidden surprises, no dramatic variations reflecting the indigenous situation. The design style, honed and perfected in a host of different locations, can be relied on to transform the landscape to a predetermined philosophy. You are playing in Kanchanaburi but equally, given the lush conditions and abundance of palm trees, you

could be playing a Nicklaus course in Palm Springs or Florida.

The course runs over a relatively level site, with areas of strategic water coming into play on just over half the holes. Open since 1991, there is a fine air of maturity in the well-established trees, flowering shrubs and formal gardening around the clubhouse, as well as the many facilities. The opening holes for each nine are a pleasant stroll just below the extensive clubhouse/hotel

veranda, giving an air of intimacy to the game. The holes flow in two gently undulating loops around land earmarked for future property development. Flowing

mounds, especially near the greens, often conceal sunken bunkers, while other large areas of waste sand await the unwary – one of the architect's trademarks. There are five tees at each hole, allowing players at all levels to appreciate the strategic challenge inherent in the demanding design.

The 8th is a tough par 5, into the prevailing wind. The split-level fairway offers a choice off the tee on a hole with water all along the right-hand side, much sand and a

Above: The clubhouse is surrounded by a wealth of shrubs and trees.

green angled out into the lake. The 12th has a similar, if even more potentially disastrous, problem. The hole is bisected by a creek that winds from tee to green. There is clear choice of play left for a reasonably safe three on, or, alternatively, you can risk water and waste sand right to a fairway offering a shot at the well-protected, angled green.

ROYAL RITUALS

As well as the Emerald Buddha (see p.24), the royal family also participates in another seasonal event, the Royal Ploughing Ceremony. This is held in May, at the approach of the rainy season, to ensure a successful harvest. The ceremony is held on a sand-covered arena by the palace in the king's presence. The ceremony features two gold-caparisoned white oxen pulling a scarlet plough being led round a series of circuits by men in antique costume, religious officials and silk-clad virgins bearing gold and silver baskets of rice and vegetable seeds. To a background of cacophonous ancient music, the seeds are ceremoniously sown and the two beasts offered a choice of food. Their selection is thought to prophesy the forthcoming rains and the success of the eventual harvest.

Evergreen Hills

Evergreen Hills Golf Club and Resort, 152 Moo 5, Thambol Rangsali, Amphur Tha-Muang, Kanchanaburi 71110
Tel: *(034) 657 130, 657 094* **Fax:** *(034) 210 3828*
Email: *sales@evergreenhillsgolfclub.com*
Location: *Route 323 from Route 4, then Route 3209*
Course: *18 holes, 6879yd/6290m, par 72*
Type of course: *Forested sloping parkland*
Designer: *Artanan Yomchinda (1992)*
Green fees: *B*
Facilities: *Golf shop, caddies, cart and equipment hire, shoe and umbrella rental, driving range, putting green, changing facilities, refreshment shelters on course, restaurant in clubhouse, on-site hotel with swimming pool, tennis, karaoke, snooker and full convention facilities*
Visitors: *Welcome, but advance telephone call suggested*

EVERGREEN HILLS

HOLE	YD	M	PAR	HOLE	YD	M	PAR
1	566	517	5	10	388	355	4
2	385	352	4	11	210	192	3
3	401	367	4	12	527	482	5
4	394	360	4	13	359	328	4
5	160	146	3	14	393	359	4
6	407	372	4	15	439	401	4
7	555	507	5	16	160	146	3
8	199	182	3	17	394	360	4
9	392	358	4	18	550	503	5
OUT	3459	3163	36	IN	3420	3127	36

6879YD • 6290M PAR 72

The name is particularly apposite for this golf club and hotel complex located something slightly over two hours from Bangkok. Tucked away in an area of forested mountains south-west of Kanchanaburi town, the imposing low-rise clubhouse and hotel complex nestles into the base of a series of verdant, tree-covered hills. From its elevated position, the clubhouse looks out over the course, which spills neatly away downhill in two quite distinct loops separated by a central area of forest.

There are a number of open, undulating holes, where water is a strategic obstacle. However, the lasting impression for the visitor is of snaking, mounded fairways tightly lined by tall evergreens, narrow slightly doglegged chutes played either gently up or downhill over the wooded slopes nearest to the clubhouse. These are the holes that live up to

the club's name and, except for the tropical temperatures, might be set in Switzerland or Alpine France.

The course is not overlong and the two nines radiate out in an almost symmetrical pattern. However, the card is somewhat unbalanced in terms of perceived difficulty, making the finish a stern test. Only two holes, the 6th and 9th, have ratings in single figures on the front nine, yet coming home, there are seven, with the closing five-hole stretch rated as strokes 8, 1, 5, 4 and 6! The 15th has an island of fairway with two

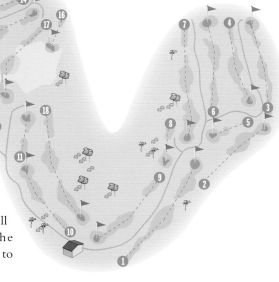

bunkers left and a substantial carry over rough to find a lozenge-shaped green with bunkers both sides. The 16th is the last short hole. It is only 160yd/146m but is across a lake to an elevated peninsula of green, steeply sloped in front and broader at the back where three curving sand traps wait. Master these two challenges and water looms again on the 17th. This turns sharply left from a raised strip of fairway to demand a long, high water-carry to a narrowing, equally elevated green protected by sand.

By comparison, the 18th should be a pushover. A mere 550yd/503m uphill, it curves narrowly left past ranks of tall trees. Encroaching rough and mounds put pressure on placement, as do four fairway bunkers. Even after finding the raised, sloping green, a par is not guaranteed.

Further up the hillside, which towers among a green cascade of trees behind the club, lies the 72-room resort hotel. It enjoys fine views out over the swimming pool, the closing holes of each nine on the course and the surrounding countryside.

Above: The 9th hole runs uphill through a funnel of trees.
Below: The 18th green finishes beneath the clubhouse.

TROPICAL GOLF TIPS

The lies are often lush and the weather humid. Take one more club than you think and, if in the rough, hit down sharply. Normally there is no pitch-and-run on Bermuda grass courses; fly the ball all the way to the green. All-weather gloves will serve you better than leather. No need for your rain gear (if it does rain, it is usually short and sharp and you will dry off in no time) but be sure to take an umbrella, ideally the silver reflective type, to ward off the sun. Also, take high-factor sun cream. Normal dress codes apply.

4 Nichigo Resort

Nichigo Resort & Country Club, 106 Moo 4, Tambol Wangdong, Amphur Muang, Kanchanaburi 71000
TEL: *(034) 518 518, 513 334* **FAX:** *(034) 518 518*
LOCATION: *From Kanchanaburi north-west Route 323; Km 10 Route 3199*
COURSE: *27 holes: Lake 3547yd/3243m; River 3566yd/3261m; Mountain 3657yd/3344m; all par 36*
TYPE OF COURSE: *Parkland in a mountain location*
DESIGNER: *Mitsuaki Kobayashi (1992)*
GREEN FEES: *BBB*
FACILITIES: *Golf shop, caddies, cart and equipment hire, shoe and umbrella rental, driving range, putting green, changing facilities, sauna, Jacuzzi, refreshment shelters on course, restaurant in clubhouse, swimming pool, karaoke, fishing, biking and other facilities including convention rooms*
VISITORS: *Welcome, but advance telephone reservation necessary*

Tucked away north-west of Kanchanaburi town, a 150-km/90-mile drive from Bangkok, this 27-hole course is laid out in an area punctuated by dramatic limestone outcrops backed by distant mountain peaks. Four of these huge rock formations, attractively clad in thick vegetation, form a backdrop to a course that offers three distinct nine-hole loops.

The Mountain nine winds gently over sloping land between and around the rocky hills, a couple of times negotiating a snaking creek that runs through the whole property. The other two courses – Lake and River - follow mostly level land beneath the mountains, where a large lake and sinuous watercourse provide the main strategic interest. This choice of golfing terrain can suit all tastes in a location of great natural beauty.

The golf course, Japanese-designed, is also under Japanese ownership and management. This is reflected in a variety of ways. The clubhouse, its long low roof set against the wooded hills, has a distinctive style. Popular Japanese dishes dominate the menu, although Thai, European and Chinese food is available. A profusion of rock and water gardens with intensive floral manicuring at every turn is the norm on the golf course, in true Japanese style. Small arched bridges, delicate hedges and neat stone borders to lakes add to the effect, although a scaled-down replica of the River Kwai bridge linking two holes on the River nine, might appear to be a touch insensitive.

The golf course is maintained in fine condition, with little serious slope built into the fairways. The large bunkers are shallow and the greens overall present level, slightly elevated targets. Apart from the obvious penalty imposed by the various water hazards, the course is not too punitive. This no doubt accounts for its appeal to a broad spectrum of

COURSE: LAKE				COURSE: RIVER				COURSE: MOUNTAIN			
HOLE	YD	M	PAR	HOLE	YD	M	PAR	HOLE	YD	M	PAR
1	424	388	4	1	431	394	4	1	410	375	4
2	543	496	5	2	380	347	4	2	558	510	5
3	410	375	4	3	180	165	3	3	153	140	3
4	186	170	3	4	574	525	5	4	448	410	4
5	427	390	4	5	438	400	4	5	443	405	4
6	404	369	4	6	407	372	4	6	220	201	3
7	573	524	5	7	411	376	4	7	585	535	5
8	175	160	3	8	198	181	3	8	416	380	4
9	405	370	4	9	547	500	5	9	424	388	4
TOTAL	3547	3243	36	TOTAL	3566	3261	36	TOTAL	3657	3344	36

3547YD • 3243M • PAR 36   3566YD • 3261M • PAR 36   3657YD • 3344M • PAR 36

Above: The Mountain nine is rich in mature trees and soaring views. Below: The lower holes are linked by delicate bridges and floral fantasy.

player. That said, there is little run on the ball and the holes play their full length, especially uphill.

Some of the most interesting (and most scenic) holes are found on the Mountain nine. After the long, uphill first, the second is an excellent dogleg right par 5. The uphill tee-shot must avoid sand both sides plus a mound on the right-hand corner that obscures the second shot. The hole then turns right and downhill past more sand, before rising to a plateau green well-protected by sand and large trees. The third requires finesse – a shortish iron across water to a shallow, angled green on the same level as the tee, faced by a stone wall that creates foreshortening and is backed by a dramatic mountain rising up behind. The next hole demands both length and accuracy, running gently downhill with thick woods all along the right-hand side and a large fairway bunker and tree left. Reaching the uphill green in two is no mean feat, but the surrounding views are great, whatever your score.

Water and sand dominate the other two nines, their holes running over relatively level ground. Perhaps the most memorable is the third on the Lake nine. This is a longish dogleg right par 4, where the approach fairway and green follow a narrow peninsula, with water on both sides.

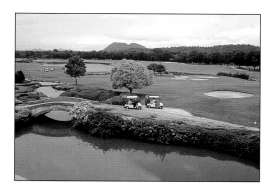

Festivals

For Thais, having fun and celebrating festivals is a key part of their lives. There is a series of local and national events held annually, most of which have been celebrated for generations. Much of Thai life, which is still primarily agricultural, is based around the seasons, and this is reflected in many of the colourful celebrations held every year. Interwoven are three of the prime factors in the traditional Thai lifestyle – an ancient history and culture, the Buddhist religion and respect for the monarchy. Festivals also represent an opportunity to dress up in exotic and colourful costumes, either to give thanks or encourage good fortune and above all, to engage in *sanuk*, otherwise, having fun.

The most important date in the year is 13 April – Songkran – although in parts of the country the celebration can last as long as two weeks. This is the traditional Thai New Year (the equivalent in many respects of Christmas in the West), when work stops and people travel home to their families. This is essentially a time for renewal – to cleanse your home and soul, to wear special new clothes and to observe rituals at the local temple. These rites include sprinkling cleansing water over images of Buddha and donating a sample of river sand to replace that removed during the year on people's shoes. It is a time to renew family relationships and, in particular, to honour the elderly with gifts and by pouring scented water over their hands. In return, they will extend wishes to the young for good luck and prosperity. There are highly colourful parades and, of particular appeal to the younger people, the extension of the water sprinkling to light-hearted drenching of passers-by, often returned in two-way liquid combat. This is all done in a spirit of fun and is especially attractive as this is the hottest month of the year.

Celebrating Songkran, where a sprinkling of water offers good luck and renewal.

Another water-related occasion of great charm is Loy Krathong, which takes place at the time of the full moon in early November, after the rains and before the harvest. Small banana leaf floats containing flowers, incense, a coin and a lighted candle are launched on the rivers by moonlight to wash away past sins and invoke good fortune. There may also be firework displays and beauty pageants.

The parade of events is seamless throughout the year. Many are linked to the land and its produce, such as the colourful Flower Festival in Chiang Mai or the Chiang Rai Lychee Fair. There are also festivals related to other fruits, including rambutan, durian and mangosteen in Rayong and Chanthaburi. Buffalo racing in Chonburi is followed by the elephant 'round-up' in Surin, where logging skills are demonstrated and also their role as caparisoned mounts in ancient warfare. Another festival sees ceremonial rockets fired to encourage rain for a plentiful harvest. Other notable events are the longboat races and dramatic light and sound events at historic Sukothai and Ayutthaya.

REGIONAL DIRECTORY

Where to Stay
Kanchanaburi

Felix River Kwai (034 515 061, Fax: 034 515 095) Nestling along the banks of the Kwai Yai River, just opposite Kanchanaburi Town, this hotel has a series of interlinked accommodation clusters. It occupies a verdant garden setting, rich in tall palm and other tropical species. There are two swimming pools, two outdoor tennis courts, a riverside jogging track, fully equipped fitness centre with massage and sauna and a snooker room. Dining is either in the Karn Café, which has both Thai and international menus, or The Good Earth restaurant, which offers Chinese food backed by attractive ethnic décor. The Green Wave Club has evening music and karaoke. The hotel is close to the River Kwai Bridge and War Cemetery, as well as the region's golf courses.

Nichigo Resort and Country Club (034 513 304, Fax: 034 513 334) This Japanese-owned golf resort (see p.118) is located a little north of Kanchanaburi Town itself. It will appeal to those who prefer to stay right on the golf course. Accommodation is in 109 simply furnished rooms in four cluster units. These are a short stroll from the golf clubhouse, where there is Thai, European and Japanese food on the menu. Guests can enjoy a swimming pool, sauna, Jacuzzi and, of course, 27 holes of scenic golf.

Below: Colourful and romantic, guests wish luck to the couple with holy water at a Thai wedding.

Where to Eat
Apart from the hotels and golf clubs in the region, the choice for the visitor is fairly limited. The **River Kwai Floating Restaurant** (034 512 842, Fax: 034 512 745) is located very close to the bridge of the same name. It offers the choice of air-conditioned dining at street level or a riverside table on the floating wooden raft below. The restaurant, which serves both Thai and Chinese food, thoughtfully provides differing set menus for Asian and European groups.

What to See
The extreme topography of the region, which caused so much hardship to the railway builders in the 1940s, now attracts nature lovers and activity enthusiasts. There are natural parks, spectacular waterfalls, river rafting and elephant trekking. Of particular interest are the **Sai Yok** waterfall and the nearby **Prasat Muang Sing** historical park, where temples from the Lopburi period 700-800 years ago are being restored. Interesting caves include the **Lawa** and **Kra Sae**, some 50km/31 miles north of Kanchanaburi. Further on are the **Erewan** waterfall and **Pra That** cave, with monumental stalactites. On a more sombre note, the **River Kwai Bridge**, still in use for trains and pedestrians, contains part of the original prisoner-of-war construction. The town has two war cemeteries, **Don Rak** and **Chonk-Kai**, containing the remains of 8732 prisoners who lost their lives working on the Railway. Nearby is the **Jeath War Museum**, a replica prisoner-of-war camp, with many relics and artefacts.

Chapter 6

Western Region

International awareness of seaside holiday destinations in Thailand tends to be concentrated on Pattaya in the east and the islands of Koh Samui and Phuket in the far south. Yet the very first beach resort in the country was created along the coast of the Gulf of Siam southwest of Bangkok at Hua Hin. This location of serene beauty has a gentle, ageless charm. Along with its more recently created sister resort of Cha-am, it also offers perhaps Thailand's finest holiday golf.

Now a three-hour drive from the capital through the historic town of Phetchaburi, this region was, until the early part of the last century, a fairly inaccessible area of small fishing villages. The European vogue for the remedial effects of spa resorts and sea air had been

Left: Watersports are popular along the coast.
Above: Quaint examples of topiary tower over golfers playing at Royal Hua Hin.

recognized by King Rama IV. This, coupled with the opening in 1916 of the southern railway line passing through Hua Hin (then known as Samoriang) on its way to Malaysia, provided the catalyst for the royal family and the elite of Bangkok to develop beach houses under the cooling breezes of Hua Hin-on-sea. Here they could escape from the oppressive heat and humidity of the hot season. The original golf course (see p.132) and the related beachside Railway Hotel began operations in 1923, paving the way for the establishment of an elegant and fashionable resort.

The twin resorts of Cha-am and Hua Hin, just 25km/15 miles further south, still have a quiet and relaxed atmosphere. The long stretches of white sand are now backed by a selection of quality hotels. The rambling old town of Hua Hin has small shops, a night market and excellent seafood restaurants perched out over the

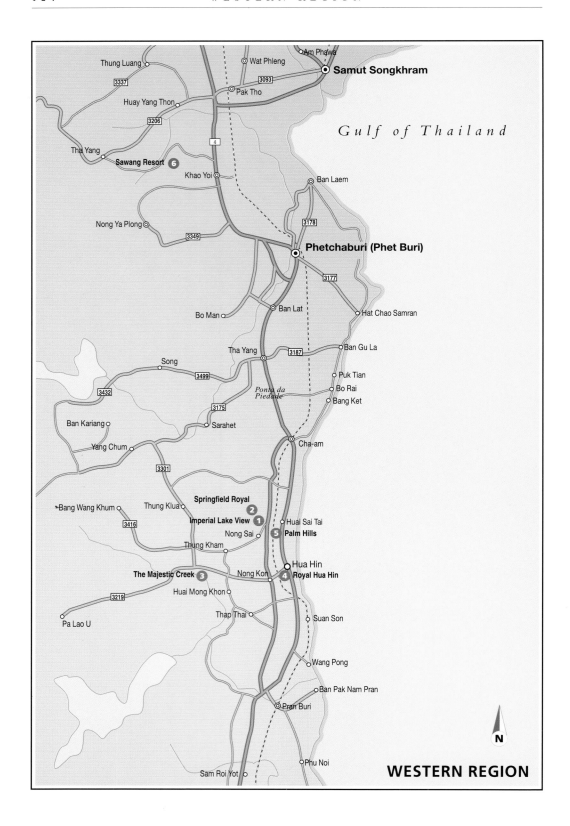

Thung Luang
3337
Huay Yang Thon
3206
Tha Yang
Sawang Resort **6**
Khao Yoi
Nong Ya Plong
3349

Wat Phleng
Am Phawa
Samut Songkhram
3093
Pak Tho
4

Gulf of Thailand

Ban Laem
3178
Phetchaburi (Phet Buri)
3177

Bo Man
Ban Lat
Hat Chao Samran

Song
Tha Yang
3187
Ban Gu La
3499
Puk Tian
3432
Ponta da Piedade
Bo Rai
3175
Bang Ket
Ban Kariang
Sarahet
Yang Chum
Cha-am
3301

Bang Wang Khum
Thung Klua
Springfield Royal
2
3416
Imperial Lake View **1**
Nong Sai
Huai Sai Tai
5 **Palm Hills**
Thung Kham

The Majestic Creek **3**
Nong Kon
Hua Hin
4 **Royal Hua Hin**
3219
Huai Mong Khon
Thap Thai
Suan Son
Pa Lao U

Wang Pong
Ban Pak Nam Pran
Pran Buri

N

Phu Noi
WESTERN REGION
Sam Roi Yot

water. This tranquil setting has much to offer the visitor. The usual drawbacks of popular tourist destinations, such as crowds, noise, nightlife and over-development have passed this region by. It has a delightful ambience, redolent of the past but supported by every modern convenience and facility.

Six fine 18-hole golf courses can be found within a 25-minute drive from Hua Hin. Each is quite different in style and difficulty, and will prove more than enough for most holiday golfers. Any visitor to the region should also try to find time to experience some of the culture and history that abounds in the area.

Start with Hua Hin railway station (right by the golf course), where a charming wooden waiting room, a confection in ochre and white, sits in splendid isolation on the platform for the exclusive use of royalty. Two royal palaces nearby are also worth a visit. King Prachadhipok built the Klai Kangwon ('Far from Worries') Palace in 1926 in Spanish style overlooking the sea as a gift for his golf-loving wife. Another is the Maruk Khatayawan golden teak palace of King Vajiravudh, an airy collection of wooden pavilions and walkways at the beach edge.

Other sights include the 11-tiered Pala-U waterfall, famous for its butterflies, and the Phraya Nakhon cave. This has an enchanting pavilion honouring King Rama V at the entrance and many Buddha images within, lit by sunlight entering through an opening above. Another town worth visiting is nearby Phetchaburi. See Khao Wang, the 'Mountain Palace' of King Rama IV, 17th-century Wat Yai Suwannaram, and Khao Luang, a dramatic cave temple.

Below: Long stretches of clear white sand edge the warm waters of the Gulf of Thailand.

Imperial Lake View

The Imperial Lake View Hotel and Golf Club, 80 Moo 4, Hubkrapong–Pranburi Road, Cha-Am, Phetchaburi 76120

TEL: *(032) 456 233-9* **FAX:** *(032) 520 098*
LOCATION: *Fork right at Km 202 (Route 4), course is a few kilometres down the road*
COURSE: *27 holes, Championship 18 6915yd/6323m, par 72; Desert 9 3417yd/3125m, par 36*
TYPE OF COURSE: *Gently undulating desert-style course, with mounding, palms, waste areas and rocks*
DESIGNER: *Roger Packard (1993 and 1997)*
GREEN FEES: *BBB*
FACILITIES: *Golf shop, caddies, cart and golf equipment hire, shoe and umbrella rental, driving range, putting green, changing facilities, Jacuzzi, on-site hotel, swimming pool, squash, tennis, snooker, refreshment shelters on course, restaurant in clubhouse*
VISITORS: *Welcome, but advance telephone call advised*

IMPERIAL LAKE VIEW

HOLE	YD	M	PAR	HOLE	YD	M	PAR
1	410	375	4	10	430	393	4
2	550	503	5	11	382	349	4
3	426	389	4	12	471	431	5
4	185	169	3	13	433	396	4
5	521	476	5	14	207	189	3
6	401	367	4	15	540	494	5
7	323	295	4	16	404	369	4
8	194	177	3	17	176	161	3
9	422	386	4	18	440	402	4
OUT	3432	3138	36	IN	3483	3185	36

6915YD • 6323M • PAR 72

In the relaxed coastal holiday area linking Cha-Am and Hua Hin, there is a good selection of very playable golf. Most courses are of fairly recent origin and each offers something quite different. Perhaps the one that will appeal to most visitors, whatever their handicap, is the layout at Lake View, now extended to 27 holes. It was designed by American Roger Packard, who later produced Lam Luk Ka near Bangkok. He has transformed an area of relatively level pineapple farms into a modern, international specification golf course. The initial 18 holes undulate past ranks of transplanted palms and strategic water hazards in an attractive, and often decep-tive, fashion. By contrast, the newer 'Desert' nine is a real challenge. It offers a complete and utter change of character, the forerunner of what should be a great golfing test when the full 18 holes are completed.

The original course is characterized by the extent of earthmoving in its creation – a trademark of the designer. With large mounding to either side, the well-defined fairways rise and fall in billowing green ribbons, like the waves of the sea. This is a most pleasant situation; the course is laid out in rolling, undulating land surrounded by distant wooded hills and one conical, rocky peak. There are many large, elevated greens, each supported by flowing mounds and attractive palm trees.

In many cases, you can choose to putt from the fringe, which is quite unusual on a Bermuda grass course. The bunkers, which are sometimes quite large and deep, are all visible

Above: The rolling slopes of the course have a mountain backdrop. Below: The open 'Desert' nine has many natural hazards.

to the player. The fairways are fairly wide; the problems lie more with the rolling nature of the land and potential sloping lies. There is no deep rough just off the fairway but pass the mounded palm trees and you probably have a lost ball, such is the nature of the penal off-course growth. Interspersed among the palm trees are other tree varieties, including mango. This is attractive golf, where the course flows in a continuous movement over rolling slopes, with few level lies and many carries over water and indigenous rushes.

Two memorable holes are the 12th and 14th. The former, a dogleg left par 5, is short enough to tempt the longer hitter to cut the corner. However, with water all along the left and in front of the sloping green, it pays to be conservative. The 14th is made, not by its length, but by all the tees being islands in a lake as is the green. The target is sizeable, but water pressure can prove a problem.

The Desert nine is, by contrast, tight and punishing. Reminiscent of courses in Arizona or California, it offers either untouched undergrowth or bare scrubland, punctuated by large rocks and cacti, just off the winding fairways. These are a delight to the eye but potentially punitive to your scorecard. A very fair and exciting test, to be treated with respect.

The hotel runs in a low-rise curve from the clubhouse round an attractive swimming pool, which itself looks directly out over the course. With a view of flowing green mounds sprinkled with palms and the blue shades of distant hills, this is a truly memorable location.

Springfield Royal

Springfield Royal Country Club, 193 Moo 6, Huay-Sai Nua, Petchkasem Road, Cha-Am, Phetchaburi 76120
TEL: *(032) 451 181* **FAX:** *(032) 451 194*
EMAIL: *info@springfieldresort.com*
LOCATION: *6km west of Regent Cha-Am Hotel via Route 4 (at Km 215)*
COURSE: *18 holes, 7063yd/6458m, par 72*
TYPE OF COURSE: *Championship-quality test over gently sloping land with many hazards*
DESIGNER: *Jack Nicklaus (1993)*
GREEN FEES: *BBB*
FACILITIES: *Pro shop, caddies, cart and golf equipment hire, shoe and umbrella rental, driving range, pitching and putting greens, teaching school, changing facilities, refreshment shelters on course, restaurant in clubhouse, beachside hotel nearby. Further 18 holes under construction*
VISITORS: *Welcome, but advance telephone call advised*

SPRINGFIELD ROYAL

HOLE	YD	M	PAR	HOLE	YD	M	PAR
1	378	346	4	10	418	382	4
2	533	487	5	11	397	363	4
3	451	412	4	12	518	474	5
4	209	191	3	13	422	386	4
5	418	382	4	14	178	163	3
6	167	153	3	15	460	421	4
7	535	489	5	16	408	373	4
8	393	359	4	17	202	185	3
9	429	392	4	18	527	482	5
OUT	3533	3230	36	IN	3530	3228	36

7063 YD • 6458M PAR 72

Many courses claim to be of international championship quality, often with little justification. However, Springfield Royal is the undoubted star of this region and its course is definitely among the best five in Thailand. It has all the features that have made any course designed by Jack Nicklaus admired and feared in equal measure. These include: length; greens heavily protected by sand that demand long, high approach shots; penal water; large tracts of waste bunker; rocks; and some areas of severe rough. However, do not let this put you off. There are five sets of tees from which to choose and there are many fine opportunities to test your game over what is a genuine golfing examination, provided you do not delude yourself that you are better than you really are.

Situated just a little further inland than the Lake View course, Springfield benefits from the same sheltering wooded hills. It has a palatial clubhouse perched up above a cascade of floral gardening and the course itself, giving excellent views over the surrounding area and eastwards to the coast. The many trees planted during its construction have matured nicely and now define the individual holes, which are kept in an excellent condition. There is a very clear differentiation on each hole between the risk-and-reward route for the better player and a safer alternative for others. The latter usually leaves a tougher approach or a more certain bogey. In many cases, a good drive on the ideal line can benefit from a favourable downslope for additional yardage, very welcome on a course that plays its full length. However, penalties lie in wait for the overambitious.

Most visitors will remember the 6th hole, a highly scenic par 3 (see photo right) across a large waste bunker and water hazard to a small green cradled within mounds and three sand traps with a mountain backdrop. Another hole that typifies the nature of the course is the demanding par 4 13th (see p.20). The 18th is in the same mould, where your drive is blind uphill on a left-hand dogleg. Players will aim to reach or pass the corner to have sight of the green, an island floating out in the lake below the clubhouse. The perfect tee shot leaves a chance to be home in two; anything else risks the water.

Given the level of quality and facilities, the cost of playing here is good value. The course is kept in superb condition, the caddies are smart and the drinks shelters welcoming. The pro shop is above average, and there is a well-respected golf school using the latest teaching aids as well as the manicured pitching and putting greens and driving range.

Above: Teeshot view of the par 3 6th hole.
Below: Holing out on the 18th green; palatial
clubhouse in rear.

The Majestic Creek

The Majestic Creek Country Club, 164 Moo 4,
Tubtai, Hua Hin, Prachuabkirikhan 77110
TEL: (032) 520 162-6 **FAX:** (032) 520 477
EMAIL: majesticgolf@thailand.com
LOCATION: 25km west from Hua Hin to Huai Mong
Khon
COURSE: 18 holes, 6961yd/6365m, par 72
TYPE OF COURSE: Undulating, well-landscaped course
with mature palms and considerable strategic water
DESIGNER: Dr Sukitti Klangvisai (1993)
GREEN FEES: BBB
FACILITIES: Golf shop, caddies, cart and golf equipment
hire, shoe and umbrella rental, driving range, pitching
and putting greens, changing facilities, refreshment
shelters on course, restaurant in clubhouse, beachside
hotel nearby
VISITORS: Welcome, but advance telephone call
advised. Dress code

THE MAJESTIC CREEK

HOLE	YD	M	PAR	HOLE	YD	M	PAR
1	421	385	4	10	374	342	4
2	345	315	4	11	418	382	4
3	373	341	4	12	234	214	3
4	157	143	3	13	578	528	5
5	547	500	5	14	363	332	4
6	140	128	3	15	405	370	4
7	388	355	4	16	450	411	4
8	447	409	4	17	145	132	3
9	588	538	5	18	588	538	5
OUT	3406	3114	36	IN	3555	3250	36

6961YD • 6365M • PAR 72

Tucked away inland some 30 minutes'
drive past rural fruit farms west from Hua
Hin, this course is a visual delight and a
pleasure to play. It is laid out below wooded
mountains, rising behind the clubhouse,
which are not only picturesque
but form the border

provides comfortable fairway lies and perfectly
acceptable, if a touch slow, putting surfaces.

After playing here, the visitor is left with
two abiding impressions. One is of flowing
fairways, which dip, roll and undulate in
sinuous, seductive fashion from one green
plateau to another, well above the level of the
many discreetly sited water hazards. The other
is of the vivid yellows, oranges, purples
and pinks of the course's abundant flowers
and flame trees. Even the creeks and ditches
have colourful touches and quaint
timber bridges; these are a treat
for the eye but do not in any
way disrupt play. There are
also plenty of palms and
other trees flanking the
mounded rim of fairways,
which are sufficiently

between Thailand and the neighbouring
country of Myanmar.

The creation of Thai golf architect Dr
Sukitti Klangvisai, this comparatively new
course is always kept in immaculate
condition. In contrast to other local courses, it
is planted with local zoysia grass, which not
only requires less feeding and water, but

Above: The short 17th, with well-defended sloping green.
Below: The view up the 18th to the clubhouse.

mature to block a wayward shot. The greens are often sloped towards the approach, with plenty of movement, mirroring the gentle undulation that marks the holes themselves. This is good, thinking golf in a delightful setting with a very natural feel to the course and its surroundings.

The final hole, 588yd/538m off the back tee, is truly memorable. From the tee, all the problems of this double-dogleg par 5 are apparent (see photo right). The drive is across a creek to an elevated plateau where the player is faced with a choice. He must either play left of a large, punitive lake to a narrow neck of fairway, where palm trees and mounded bunkers lurk, or, if his ball is long enough and has avoided the lake and another bunker right, he can go for broke to an angled green across the water and more sand. A great hole, offering a challenging finish to a satisfying test of golf.

The clubhouse has recently been renovated. It now offers extensive, well-fitted locker rooms, a large golf shop and both air-conditioned indoor and terrace outdoor dining. In addition, a further nine holes are now under construction.

Situated down by the sea and close to town, the Majestic Beach Resort also offers golfing visitors attractive accommodation under the same ownership as the golf club. There are 48 rooms, each with an ocean view. The resort also has a free-form swimming pool and a high level of friendly, personal service.

Royal Hua Hin

Royal Hua Hin Golf Course, Damnernkasem Road,
Hua Hin, Prachuabkirikhan 77110
TEL: *(032) 512 473-4* **FAX:** *(032) 513 038*
LOCATION: *Alongside Hua Hin railway station*
COURSE: *18 holes, 6678yd/6106m, par 72*
TYPE OF COURSE: *Mature traditional parkland*
running towards and up a wooded mountainside
DESIGNER: *A.O. Robins (1924)*
GREEN FEES: *BB*
FACILITIES: *Golf shop, caddies, golf equipment hire,*
shoe and umbrella rental, driving range, putting green,
tuition, changing facilities, refreshment shelters on course,
restaurant in clubhouse, hotel nearby .
VISITORS: *Welcome, but advance telephone call advised*

ROYAL HUA HIN

HOLE	YD	M	PAR	HOLE	YD	M	PAR
1	569	520	5	10	356	325	4
2	384	351	4	11	565	517	5
3	535	489	5	12	305	279	4
4	155	142	3	13	356	325	4
5	131	120	3	14	149	136	3
6	444	406	4	15	564	516	5
7	385	352	4	16	198	181	3
8	332	303	4	17	413	378	4
9	397	363	4	18	440	402	4
OUT	3332	3047	35	IN	3346	3060	36

6678YD • 6106M • PAR 72

Playing here is like stepping into some form of time capsule; this is living history and an experience that no serious golfer should miss. The course was the first purpose-built holiday golf course in Thailand. It was created by royal command during the reign of King Rama VI and has been in play since 1924. The seaside resort of Hua Hin had been a regular retreat of the royal family and the social elite in the hot season, giving them a chance to escape the humidity of Bangkok and relax under the cool breezes off the Gulf of Siam. Golf, as a pastime for royalty, the wealthy and the well connected, had become increasingly popular in fashionable European summer spa resorts including Deauville, Dinard, Le Touquet, Biarritz, Cannes and Monte Carlo.

Limited facilities for the game existed only in the capital, supported by the royal family and the expatriate community. The king felt that golf should be available in Hua Hin. HRH Prince Kampaengpetch Akarayothin, then Director General of the Royal State Railway Department, asked A. O. Robins, a Scottish engineer responsible for the railway in Phetchaburi, to design a nine-hole course. Mr Robins, clearly a golfer himself, must have been a man of considerable foresight and vision. The game at that time was generally played over any level land available, not unlike some of the original seaside links in Scotland, mainly due to the considerable difficulty of earthmoving and reshaping. In the days before bulldozers, there was only a horse or buffalo-drawn scraper and the hand of man for landscaping.
A. O. Robins

took on the challenge of land sloping up from the coastal railway line into the surrounding hills and some quite steeply wooded mountainside – revolutionary at the time.

This is golf created with a feel for the terrain, designed by the eye rather than the tractor. The result is ageless, with some fine, natural parkland-style holes that have withstood the test of time. The early nine holes became 18 in 1925 (5601yd/5121m – par 75). Although now extended, they still provide an excellent challenge.

This is classic old-style golf, nearly 80 years in play, following the lie of the land, and kept in good condition with excellent greens. Expect small raised tees, elevated, often steeply sloping greens, shallow bunkers and sharp mounds. There are also many pleasant touches, such as topiary of animals and birds, a temple rising from the trees behind the par 3

Below: The ageless charm of this golf course is shown in the very natural layout of each hole, running up and into the richly wooded hills.

THE GRACIOUS *WAI*

Thais do not normally shake hands as a greeting, they *wai*. This charming, graceful gesture not only typifies the nature of the Thai, but serves to convey a range of meanings depending on who is involved. The *wai*, placing both palms together with the fingers upwards, accompanied by lowering the head and body, is both greeting and also a mark of respect, with a strict protocol accompanying it, depending on age, seniority or social status.

14th, a tree growing in a bunker and the ancient locomotive stranded between the railway station and the 1st tee. From the higher holes, there are splendid views back down over the course and its many mature trees to the sparkling ocean beyond.

The large airy clubhouse is unpretentious. It offers excellent service and maintains much of the original atmosphere of this pioneering and genuinely 'Royal' golf club.

 **Palm Hills**

Palm Hills Golf Resort & Country Club, 1444 Petchkasem Road, Cha-Am, Phetchaburi 76120
TEL: *(032) 520 800-11* **FAX:** *(032) 520 820*
LOCATION: *Km 222 Petchkasem Highway, Route 4 between Hua Hin and Cha-Am*
COURSE: *18 holes, 6892yd/6302m, par 72*
TYPE OF COURSE: *Gently undulating parkland with mature trees, many lakes and sea views*
DESIGNER: *Max Wexler (1992)*
GREEN FEES: *BBB*
FACILITIES: *Golf shop, caddies, cart and golf equipment hire, shoe and umbrella rental, driving range, putting green, changing facilities, refreshment shelters on course, restaurant in clubhouse, country club with swimming pool, badminton, tennis, squash, snooker, table tennis, gym, sauna, children's playground, fishing club*
VISITORS: *Welcome, but advance telephone call advised*

Holiday golfers tend to have fond memories of this course. It combines some very attractive but not overly demanding golf with exceptional views, a wealth of floral colour and natural background plus many additional sports and leisure facilities for any non-golfers in the

Above: Approach to the par 4 18th hole with the sheltered, attractive clubhouse beyond.

party. A series of wooded hills virtually surrounds the course as well as many rocky outcrops encrusted with trees. The holes are a playable length for the average visitor and the course is well cared for, especially the broad, inviting greens. Plentiful water hazards do not seriously affect play and provide an opportunity for dramatic displays of rocks and flowers. The bunkers are shallow and gently mounded, the fairways broad and there is little movement in the receptive greens, giving an altogether natural, unmanufactured appearance. This is a course where the gardening is as much a pleasure as the golf.

The clubhouse, occupying a mountain spur between the two nines, contradicts the seeming national obsession for marble palaces. It is low-rise, has attractive wooden décor, a comfortable restaurant and feels like a golf club. The welcome is as refreshing as the ice cold towels at the end of your round.

6 *Sawang Resort*

Sawang Resort Golf Club, 99 Moo 2, Khao Yoi,
Phetchaburi 76140
TEL: *(032) 499 555-7* **FAX:** *(032) 499 555*
LOCATION: *3km west of Khao Yoi, Route 4*
COURSE: *18 holes, 6959yd/6363m, par 72*
TYPE OF COURSE: *Gently undulating parkland with a*
fair amount of strategic water
DESIGNER: *Isao Katsumata (1993)*
GREEN FEES: *BB*
FACILITIES: *Golf shop, caddies, cart and golf equipment*
hire, shoe and umbrella rental, driving range, putting
green, changing facilities, refreshment shelters on course,
restaurant in clubhouse, swimming pool, accommodation
in fairway lodges
VISITORS: *Welcome, but advance telephone call advised*

Just over an hour's drive south-west from Bangkok, this club occupies a peaceful location in a natural valley backed by mountain views, little cones, peaks and limestone crags, with wooded slopes leading down to the course and its many water hazards. From a high vantage point, the front nine slopes gently downhill past lakes and mature mango trees to an inland plateau; the second loop lies over level land north of the clubhouse. This is a course to appeal to the higher handicapper, with very broad fairways, shallow bunkers and level greens in fine condition. Almost old-fashioned in some respects, it offers elevated teeing areas and flat, raised greens with little problem in between, providing that one plays away from the water hazards present on 12 of the holes.

The final three holes are the best. The 16th is a 198-yd/181-m par 3 across water and sand to a green promontory; the 17th, a 407-yd/372-m dogleg par 4, has sand and water both sides of a narrowing fairway with more water to carry just before the green. Water also holds the key on the 18th. This 508-yd/464-m par 5 has water 230yd/210m off the back tee and more all the way up the right side of an uphill finish.

Below: Teeshot view up the water-rimmed par 5 18th
with the clubhouse complex behind.

Golf by Design

In 1970, although golf had long been played in the kingdom, Thailand had no golf courses of international calibre. The 30-odd courses that existed were often fairly rustic, locally created and under the control of the military or another government agency. In most Western golfing countries, where the game had been played since the previous century or even earlier, courses of quality were commonplace. Far from being a disadvantage, however, this situation has allowed Thailand to benefit from new concepts in golf architecture and design as well as modern construction technology. Thailand is now at the forefront of those countries offering top-quality golf in resort locations and is a major contender in the holiday golf market.

The first fruits of this golfing revolution were sown near Pattaya in 1971 with Siam Country Club, in 1972 at The Rose Garden but, most significantly, with the construction

Above: Sinuous shapes of sand and mounds at Panya Park's par 3 3rd hole B course.

in 1973 of Navatanee, a modern championship layout built specifically for the 1975 World Cup. The real explosion in golf-course creation, however, came in 1990-96, when golf clubs sprouted like mushrooms throughout the country to cater to an emerging market of Thai golf enthusiasts (now numbering more than 300,000). Many were constructed in holiday areas, and most

were designed by world-class golf architects. From being in a golfing backwater, Thailand was suddenly an important player, with nearly 200 available courses, the majority newly built to international standards.

Top names in course design have produced golf to savour, perfectly maintained in ideal growing conditions. They include: Robert Trent Jones Jr – who has followed Navatanee with a number of other fine courses– Jack Nicklaus, Ronald Fream, Dennis Griffiths, Roger Packard, Jim Engh, Peter W. Thomson, Arthur Hills, Nick Faldo, Greg Norman, Gary Player, and the Dye family among others. Local designers have also made their mark, including Dr Sukitti Klangvisai, Pirapon Namatra, Dr Sukhum Sukapan-potharam, Visudh Junnanont and Artanan Yomchinda. All in all, Thailand offers world-class golf courses, often in spectacular settings – a holiday golfer's dream. With tropical weather, and a predictable rain season, Thailand has ideal growing conditions. Courses are sown with hybrid Bermuda grass and greens of Tifdwarf or, more recently, Tifeagle. In most regions, the high water table produces many water hazards and all major courses have fully automatic watering systems. Modern construction methods allow courses to stay open all year round.

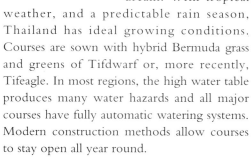

REGIONAL DIRECTORY

Where to Stay
Cha-Am
Dusit Resort & Polo Club (032 520 009, Fax: 032 520 296) This most elegant 300-room beachfront hotel is a jewel in the Dusit crown. It manages to combine a level of upmarket quality with the essential informality and unobtrusive service required of a seaside resort of this calibre. From the popular Palm Court restaurant, golden carp highlight a series of glistening pools which descend, fringed by palms, to swimming areas, a Jacuzzi, a lake with fountain and finally to the unspoiled sandy beach. Supporting a deserved reputation, the Dusit kitchens provide Royal Thai cuisine in the pool-side Ban Benjarong, authentic Italian at San Marco al fresco, European at the more formal Ascot and down near the beach, barbecued seafood at Rim Talay. There is also a fitness centre, tennis, squash, horseriding and watersports.

Hua Hin
Royal Garden Resort (032 511 881-4, Fax: 032 512 422) Just a short walk south of town leads you into a lush garden location nudging the fringe of a white-sand beach. Without compromising on quality and service, this excellent hotel manages to achieve a relaxed and peaceful ambience seemingly away from it all. There is plenty to whet your appetite, from the US steakhouse to the Italian pavilion on the beach; from the Garden Café, with a menu that ranges from Chinese to Mexican plus international dishes, to the truly authentic classic cuisine in Sala Thai. Golfers will appreciate the Sand Trap Bar plus the practice driving net. Other sports facilities include a large pool with swim-up bar, tennis, volleyball, petanque, outdoor fitness centre and Thai massage.

    Hotel Sofitel Central (032 512 021-38, Fax: 032 511 014) Golf historians will find much to admire in what was the original Railway Hotel, built in conjunction with the Hua Hin golf course. It has been totally renovated and extended in a magnificent garden setting, with unique topiary, along the edge of the beach. This luxury hotel has carefully preserved much of its heritage, including a small museum, where high tea is served. Timeless elegance is reflected in the rich teakwood, marble, silks and crystal. Dining ranges from classic French to fresh seafood and authentic Thai. Golf, naturally, is on the doorstep, but there is also a large free-form pool, tennis, putting greens, badminton, billiards and croquet.

    Chiva-Som International Health Resort (032 536 536, Fax: 032 511 154) offers something completely different. The essence of this secluded, relaxed location is to switch off and rejuvenate, aided by a wide range of treatments, exercise, hydrotherapy, beauty treatments and spa cuisine. The Japanese décor, Thai-style teak buildings, quiet water features and restrained seaside setting form a treatment in themselves.

Where to Eat
Hua Hin and its near neighbour Cha-Am give a clear dining choice. The considerable number of high-class hotels spread along the coastline offer excellent dining with a broad selection of international menus. In contrast, Hua Hin, still in many respects the seaside village of old, offers small, friendly establishments with good food at reasonable prices. Several fresh fish and seafood restaurants hover invitingly on timber platforms over the sea, providing a romantic setting under the tropical stars. Back towards town, Italian, Swiss, French, Mexican, American steak and Thai restaurants compete for your custom. There are also a number of unpretentious expatriate pubs.

What to See
In many respects, the prime attraction of the Hua Hin area is its lack of man-made sights and entertainments. Its inherent charm lies in the long stretches of unspoiled beach, relative lack of sophistication, excellent golf courses and history as a holiday retreat for Thailand's royal family since the 1920s. Evidence of the latter is apparent in the charming old wooden railway station just across from the golf course, with its small *sala* for royal travellers, and the nearby Sofitel hotel, which still offers many echoes of its historic past. Not far away are the Spanish-style **Klai Kangwon** (Far from Worries) **Palace**, built by King Prachadhipok overlooking the sea. Another superb example of Thai craftsmanship is the golden teak palace of King Vajiravudh, the **Maruk Khatayawan**. Natural attractions include the **Phraya Nakhon** cave, with its enchanting royal pavilion and Buddha images, and the 11-tiered **Pala-U** waterfall, famous for its butterflies. Historic **Phetchaburi** (65km/40 miles north) is also worth a visit. A key point on the trading route from the Andaman Sea to Ayutthaya, it has some fine examples of ancient temples, many with important murals. A literal high point for visitors is the Mountain Palace of Khao Wang, built by King Rama IV in the middle of the 19th century with many beautiful buildings. A further attraction is the Khao Luang cave, with enormous stalactites and many Buddha images.

Chapter 7

Southern Region

Thailand's south is a narrow, meandering neck of land, flanked in part by the lower tip of Myanmar, working its way down below the beaches of the western coast to connect with the northern border of Malaysia. It includes a number of vacation islands, most notably Koh Samui. However, for golfing visitors there are really only two destinations. These are the popular holiday island of Phuket (which is actually connected by a causeway to the mainland) and the commercial city of Hat Yai, which is close to the Malaysian border, along with its nearby seaside resort of Songkhla. Both of these locations fall into what is popularly termed the lower south. The former eases into the Andaman Sea, while the latter faces the

Gulf of Thailand. With the proximity to Malaysia, there is a substantial Muslim and Chinese population, creating distinct differences in culture and cuisine. There are only two seasons – hot (from November to April) and rainy for the rest of the year.

In many respects, the region fulfils an escapist dream of tropical paradise. There are lush green islands with sparkling palm-fringed sandy beaches, peaceful lagoons and coral reefs rich with colourful marine life, quaint stilted fishing villages, unique hand-painted boats, towering limestone outcrops, thickly wooded green mountains and dramatic waterfalls, all in contrast with the quaint residue of history. Picturesque buildings from former times flank both ancient temples and mosques, while the often quite mountainous landscape is punctuated with rubber plantations and the azure lakes of former tin mines.

Left: The limestone formations thrusting out of Phang Nga Bay are dramatically beautiful. Above: One of many isolated white beaches.

Phuket is Thailand's largest island, 862km/536 miles – a one-hour flight – south of Bangkok. It served as a convenient stopover for early seafarers on the route between India and China. Due to the discovery of vast tin reserves both here and in the nearby province of Phangnga, it became a trading point for the Dutch, Portuguese, French and English. It resisted colonization, most notably by the Burmese in the late 18th century, in a heroic action led by two sisters. This event is commemorated by a landmark statue at a major crossroads in the centre of Phuket.

Today, the island is a green, largely mountainous, magnet for tourists. Its coastline is punctuated by a series of white-sand coves and beaches with a broad selection of hotels and a full range

Below: A boat ride north of Phuket island, the sheer limestone cliffs, rich vegetation and clear warm water attract many visitors.

of related facilities (including six excellent golf courses) to support the holiday industry. As well as rubber, coconuts, cashews and pineapples, local farming relates to the sea, with fishing, prawn and pearl farms predominant. Phuket is reckoned to provide the most succulent seafood in the land, in particular the Phuket lobster. Locals even hold an annual Seafood Festival in May.

Apart from golf, there is much to see and do in Phuket, depending on your interests and inclinations. A wildlife forest park preserves monkey, deer, bears, wild boar, gibbon and many species of bird in their natural habitat, while several protected beaches have coral reefs and are home to sea turtles. There is a full range of watersports available on the island. For those in a less active mood, there is an aquarium, butterfly and orchid farms, a museum, and a number of historic temples, particularly Pra Nahng Sahng and Pra Tong. Boat excursions can be

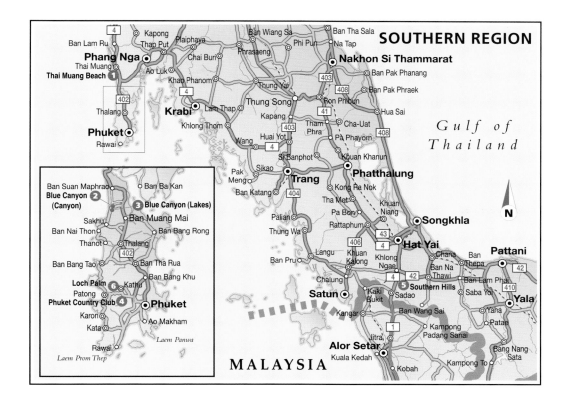

made to the unique limestone formations and caves in Phang Nga Bay or to the Phi Phi islands in nearby Krabi province as well as a 'shell graveyard' composed of fossilized shells 40 million years old.

Hat Yai, some 100km/62 miles further south, is the commercial hub of the region and gateway to Malaysia. The cosmopolitan city offers a variety of shopping opportunities, eclectic cuisine, considerable nightlife and – a local speciality – monthly encounters between fighting bulls. Just a 30-minute drive away is the tranquil seaside resort of Songkhla. This was once a pirate stronghold but is now a laid-back location with white, sandy beaches, popular seafood restaurants, a thriving fishing fleet and a fairly rustic nine holes of golf along the pine-fringed edge of the 3-km/2-mile Samila beach.

SILVER SCREEN SETTINGS

Many international film companies use Thailand's superb scenery for location shooting every year. Much in demand are the idyllic, often untouched locations in the south, offering palm-fringed crescents of sparkling white sand lapped by an azure-emerald sea with lush green mountains towering up behind. One of the best-known films shot in Thailand is the James Bond adventure *The Man with the Golden Gun* starring Roger Moore and Christopher Lee. This was partly filmed on a Phang Nga island, Kao Tapoo (now a tourist attraction) in the 1970s. More recently, and more ecologically controversial, was *The Beach*, starring Leonardo DiCaprio. This was shot in the Phi Phi archipelago of neighbouring Krabi province.

Thai Muang Beach

Thai Muang Beach Golf Course, 157/12 Moo 9,
Limdul Road, Thai Muang, Phang Nga 82120
TEL: *(076) 571 533-4* **FAX:** *(076) 571 214*
LOCATION: *35km north of Phuket International airport*
into Phang Nga province
COURSE: *18 holes, 7019yd/6418m, par 72*
TYPE OF COURSE: *Relatively level exposed seaside*
course with severe mounding, elevated greens and strategic
water
DESIGNER: *Dye Design Inc (1994)*
GREEN FEES: *BBBBB*
FACILITIES: *Golf shop, caddies, cart and golf equipment*
hire, shoe and chair and umbrella rental, driving range,
putting green, changing facilities, on-site chalets with
swimming pool, water sports, refreshment shelters on
course, bar and restaurant in clubhouse
VISITORS: *Welcome, but advance telephone call advised*

THAI MUANG

HOLE	YD	M	PAR	HOLE	YD	M	PAR
1	405	370	4	10	464	424	4
2	363	332	4	11	211	193	3
3	448	410	4	12	332	303	4
4	612	560	5	13	625	571	5
5	320	293	4	14	466	426	4
6	158	144	3	15	330	302	4
7	415	379	4	16	549	502	5
8	156	143	3	17	178	163	3
9	524	479	5	18	463	423	4
OUT	3401	3110	36	IN	3610	3300	36

7019 YD • 6418M • PAR 72

There is little doubting the near perfect conditions for holiday golf in Thailand – climate, course condition, caddies, low costs and immense charm. The only immeasurable factor is timing and a number of new golf course projects suffered, particularly where linked to real estate sales, in the downturn in the local economy a few years ago. One project with all the right credentials is the Thai Muang Beach Resort, unfortunately launched at an inopportune time and only now being discovered by the international market.

Just half-an-hour north of Phuket International airport over the Sarasin Bridge into Phang Nga, the course occupies a peaceful area of lagoons and creeks right next to a long white stretch of beach fronting the ocean. A former tin-mining property, it has water in abundance and what is planned to become an idyllic resort location. The 18-hole golf

course, built to a championship specification, is well in place along with a fine sea-facing clubhouse and a beach chalet complex. To follow are two deluxe hotels, a golf lodge, marina club, spa and fitness centre, watersports lagoon and picnic park. It is rare to find a new golf course in a seaside location of such potential; it is even rarer to find one with a finishing hole literally running along the beach, open to the gentle breezes off the Andaman Sea – something unique in Thailand.

The golf course, which was laid out over very level land that winds its way past the lakes and creeks found in this location, was created by Dye Design Inc, a

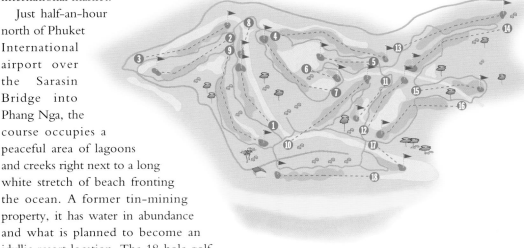

Above: Timber reinforcement and colourful flowers are features. Below: The essentially flat location is relieved by large mounds and lakes.

highly experienced team from the USA, with such coastal courses as Harbour Town at Hilton Head and Kiawah Island (of Ryder Cup fame) to their credit. They have designed a genuine golfing examination, tough off the back tees to nominated landing areas, and attractive and essentially fair from further forward. This is, without any doubt, one of the best three courses in the Southern region. However, possibly in an attempt to inject some movement into what was a very level site and to give a links feeling to this seaside course, large mounds and swales have been introduced, often next to well-elevated greens. Along with the Dye trademarks of chisel edges, flat bunker floors and liberal use of railway sleepers, these features are essentially unnatural and out of

sympathy with what is a delightful location for holiday play.

As befits a championship test, the closing holes are memorable. The 17th, known as 'The Lady', is a par 3 across water to a sliver of green that angles narrowly away from the tee, with more water beyond and behind (see p.21). It is followed by 'The Gem', a tough par 4 final hole of 463yd/423m running straight along the edge of the beach, and played to an undulating, steeply elevated green.

Blue Canyon (Canyon)

Bllue Canyon Country Club, 165 Moo 1, Thepkasattri Road, Maikaw, Thalang, Phuket 83140
TEL: *(076) 327 440* **FAX:** *(076) 327 449*
EMAIL: *reservation@bluecanyonclub.com*
LOCATION: *2km south of Phuket airport, Route 402*
COURSE: *Canyon Course 18 holes, 7119yd/6510m, par 72 (also Lakes Course; see p.146)*
TYPE OF COURSE: *Championship-level parkland running over wooded hillside and around and across large water hazards*
DESIGNER: *Yoshikazu Kato (1991)*
GREEN FEES: *BBBBB*
FACILITIES: *Golf shop, caddies, golf equipment, shoe and umbrella hire, golf school, driving range, pitching and putting greens, changing facilities, sauna, steam rooms, Jacuzzi, massage, fitness room, golfers' lodge, swimming pool, tennis courts, refreshment shelters on course, restaurant and terrace coffee shop in clubhouse*
VISITORS: *Welcome – no restrictions, but advance telephone call advised*

BLUE CANYON (CANYON)

HOLE	YD	M	PAR	HOLE	YD	M	PAR
1	380	347	4	10	392	358	4
2	218	199	3	11	600	549	5
3	449	410	4	12	440	402	4
4	368	336	4	13	390	357	4
5	398	364	4	14	194	177	3
6	556	508	5	15	586	536	5
7	204	186	3	16	357	326	4
8	402	367	4	17	221	202	3
9	561	513	5	18	403	368	4
OUT	3536	3233	36	IN	3583	3276	36

7119 YD • 6510M • PAR 72

This is probably one of Thailand's best-known golfing locations, mainly due to worldwide television exposure of two Johnnie Walker Classic events in 1994 and 1998, won by Greg Norman and Tiger Woods respectively. Planned as an exclusive private country club with two top-class golf courses and other facilities for well-heeled members and residents, it is currently open to visitors. Although not cheap, it offers a unique golfing experience. Sited only a few minutes from the international airport, it occupies two secluded, sloping, wooded valleys, linked by a central spur of higher ground. The holes filter down to a series of clear freshwater lakes, which tin mining created for golf.

The two courses (the second, Lakes, opened in 1999) were designed by Japanese golf architect Yoshikazu Kato. He has

taken considerable care to preserve the natural environment. In splendid Japanese tradition, he ensured that off-course horticulture includes cascading waterfalls, rock gardens and a profusion of bright, colourful flowers. The Canyon course finishes directly under the clubhouse and makes good use of changes of elevation in the land as well as existing rubber and other trees plus dramatic carries over and around the two primary water hazards. In common with many championship venues, the most notable holes appear in the second nine. The 13th (see photo lower right) is a right-angled pure 'risk and reward' par 4 across the gaping depths of the canyon. It is followed by one of the most photographed

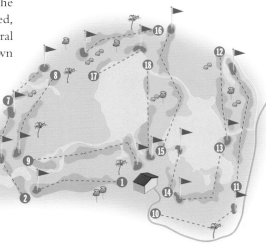

(and feared) short holes in Asia, with the green a curving teardrop floating in the water below the elevated tees (see p.21). The 17th, 221yd/202m downhill to an L-shaped green hugging the lake rim, has been ranked one of the best 500 holes in the world. The par 4 18th, although not long by professional standards, has a very narrow landing area for the drive (see photo right), tilted towards the lake which follows the fairway edge.

The three-level clubhouse dominates the central spur, offering superb views over the course. Two restaurants serve Thai, Chinese, Japanese or Continental fare, while the pro shop is elegantly comprehensive in what it offers. The spacious locker rooms are a feast of teak and leather, offering the luxury of two saunas, five spas and a Jacuzzi.

Right: The clubhouse view of the narrow 18th, where water plays a key role.
Below: Driving across the lake and canyon rim at the dogleg right, par 4 13th hole.

Blue Canyon (Lakes)

Blue Canyon Country Club, 165 Moo 1, Thepkassatri Road, Maikaw, Thalang, Phuket 83140
TEL: *(076) 327 440* **FAX:** *(076) 327 449*
EMAIL: *reservation@bluecanyonclub.com*
LOCATION: *2km south of Phuket airport, Route 402*
COURSE: *Lakes Course 18 holes, 7129yd/6519m, par 72 (also Canyon course; see p.144)*
TYPE OF COURSE: *Thinking man's test over sloping wooded land with much strategic water*
DESIGNER: *Yoshikazu Kato (1999)*
GREEN FEES: *BBBBB*
FACILITIES: *Golf shop, caddies, golf equipment, shoe and umbrella hire, golf school, driving range, pitching and putting greens, changing facilities, sauna, steam rooms, Jacuzzi, massage, fitness room, golfers' lodge, swimming pool, tennis courts, refreshment shelters on course, restaurant and terrace coffee shop in clubhouse*
VISITORS: *Welcome – no restrictions, but advance telephone call advised*

This is the newer of the two courses and it certainly lives up to its name. The holes flow over a sloping hillside that runs down to a connected series of lakes. These feature in all but one of the holes, sometimes on both sides of slender fairways. It forms a nice contrast with the Canyon, being a bit shorter but highly strategic; placement off the tee is everything. There are few bunkers; with this much water they become superfluous. Each hole is different and very interesting, with some severe doglegs and good use of trees. Both courses are kept in excellent condition, with perfect fairway lies.

The final hole on the Lakes, 471yd/431m uphill par 4, is a real killer. With water in play left from the tee and a narrowing fairway, the approach to an elevated, well-bunkered green over water will test the best.

Nearby is the fully equipped Golf School, while back at the centrally sited clubhouse, the 49-room Golfers' Lodge offers elegant accommodation with unrivalled golf course balcony views.

Below: The view from behind the elevated 18th green reveals the narrow fairway and extent of unseen water hazard that defines this tough par 4.

Phuket Country Club

*Phuket Country Club, Old Course, 80/1 Moo 5,
Vichitsongkram Road, Kathu, Phuket 83120*
TEL: *(076) 321 038-40* **FAX:** *(076) 321 721*
*Phuket Country Club, Country Club Course, 97/4
Vichitsongkram Road, Kathu, Phuket 83120*
TEL: *(076) 321 365-71* **FAX:** *(076) 321 372*
LOCATION: *Route 4020, Km 7 Vichitsongkram Road*
COURSE: *27 holes, Old Course 18 holes
6484yd/5929m, par 72; Country Club Course 9 holes
3575yd/3269m, par 37*
TYPE OF COURSE: *Old – mixture of rolling slopes,
level parkland and lakeside holes to suit all levels;
Country Club – tight and demanding with much water
(maximum 24 handicap recommended)*
DESIGNER: *Dr Sukitti Klangvisai (1989)*
GREEN FEES: *Old BBBBB; Country Club BB*
FACILITIES: *Clubhouse at each course, golf shop,
caddies, golf equipment, shoe hire, driving range, putting
greens, golf tuition, changing facilities, sauna, swimming
pool, tennis, snooker, refreshment shelters on course, bar
and restaurants in clubhouse*
VISITORS: *Welcome, but advance reservation necessary.
Soft spikes*

This was the first modern golf course in
Phuket and the first to make use of the
large lakes left from former tin mines. The
main (Old) course essentially surrounds one
huge lake, with challenging water carries and
plenty of sand. Its relatively short length and
superb condition make it popular with golfers
at all levels. The newer nine-hole course close
by, with its own clubhouse, good restaurant
and a fully equipped recreation centre and
driving range, is considerably more demanding,
with water in play 90 per cent of the time.

Most visitors come away with two
memories. First, the amazing level of
gardening, with spectacular shrubs and a blaze
of colourful flowers at every turn. Also the
10th hole on the Old Course, a 557-yd/
509-m sharp dogleg right par 5 around the
main lake, where a drive with carry of over
240yd/219m could take the direct route
over water to be on the green in one.

*Below: A wealth of mature trees and undulating, clearly
defined holes are among the key features of the popular and
well-established Old Course.*

 Southern Hills

Southern Hills Golf & Country Club, 128 Moo 8,
Kanchanavanich Rd. (Highway Hat Yai–Sadao),
Banphu, Hat Yai, Songkhla 90110
TEL: (074) 343 560-3, (01) 609 3385 **FAX:** (074)
343 564
EMAIL: shills@hadyai.loxinfo.co.th
WWW: southernhillsgolf.com
LOCATION: Km 40 on Route 4 south of Hat Yai city
COURSE: 18 holes, 7045yd/6442m, par 72
TYPE OF COURSE: Modern layout following a river
valley
DESIGNER: Dye Design Inc (1999)
GREEN FEES: BBB; closed Tuesdays
FACILITIES: Golf shop, caddies, cart and equipment
rental, shoe and umbrella hire, pitching and putting
green, changing facilities, catering in clubhouse, 30-room
lakeside resort planned with swimming pool, snooker and
fitness centre
VISITORS: Welcome, but telephone reservation suggested

Southern Hills is the latest addition to the
Thai golfing scene and offers a dramatic,
demanding test of the game in a beautiful
setting. Just 15 minutes from central Hat Yai,
it undulates along a narrow, winding river
valley flanked on both sides by thick jungle.
Further back are former rubber plantations set
below ranks of wooded hills. The valley
location essentially controls the shape and
nature of the course, with the holes laid out
on either side of the water. The front nine
goes out and returns on one side of the
attractive central, tropical-style clubhouse; the
back nine does the same in the opposite
direction. Still in the early stages of
development, this is a golfing resort location
that should easily rank among the top dozen
in the country.

SOUTHERN HILLS

HOLE	YD	M	PAR	HOLE	YD	M	PAR
1	359	328	4	10	369	337	4
2	421	385	4	11	415	379	4
3	178	163	3	12	567	518	5
4	440	402	4	13	309	282	4
5	608	556	5	14	199	182	3
6	406	371	4	15	425	389	4
7	334	305	4	16	541	495	5
8	200	183	3	17	218	199	3
9	583	533	5	18	473	432	4
OUT	3529	3227	36	IN	3516	3215	36

7045YD • 6442M • PAR 72

The course is the work of American Perry
O. Dye. His other effort in this region is Thai
Muang Beach, which is another fine and
attractive test. An architect with a highly
distinctive style and a penchant for moving the
existing land to suit it, he has had to accept, in
this case, the constraints of the location. In so
doing, he has produced an interesting and
highly playable golf course, although somewhat
demanding when played from the back tees.
Huge chisel-edged mounds guard the
fairway flanks away from the
water, concealing flat-floored
bunkers and strong slopes.
By the river itself, much
natural flora increases
the problem. The
excellent greens
have plenty of
movement,
often
throwing
the ball the
wrong side of a
ridge or mound.
On the outward half,
the 4th asks the first real
questions. The drive must thread
between sand right and the river on the left,
leaving an approach to a rolling green set
across the river left through trees, with a

Above: The 18th green with sand and an attractive waterfall behind. Below: Steep mounding beside the fairways is a trademark of the designer.

bunker behind. With considerable vegetation and water to carry, a clear choice must be made. The 8th is 200yd/183m across a chasm of water and jungle to a green framed by tropical trees and a large bunker.

Coming home, there is the signature 17th, with the Dye island green, followed by what could well be the toughest finishing hole in the country. Its 473yd/432m curve sharply around a lake, offering two levels of fairway and a series of angular mounds down the right-hand side instead of sand. The second is played to a green edging the water left, guarded by mounded sand right and a scenic waterfall behind – truly memorable.

Southern Hills brings a breath of fresh air to the far south, a challenging and very attractive golf resort of true class.

Thai Food

One of the greatest delights of Thailand is the local cuisine. It is colourful and aromatic – an event for the eye as well as the palate. Dishes vary from region to region, but are usually accompanied by fragrant rice, often steamed. The wide array of dishes are based mainly on pork, chicken, fish and seafood, supported by a wealth of fresh vegetables. Rich flavours are created from a palette of exotic herbs and spices, including kaffir lime leaves, coriander, lemongrass, holy basil, bay leaf, lime and a selection of chillies. Coconut milk is often added, particularly in curries, while fish sauce (*nam pla*) or shrimp paste add saltiness. A meal is usually a communal occasion where a number of dishes are served together for all to share. A typical meal might feature a soup with several stir-fried, steamed or grilled dishes and the inevitable rice. Thai desserts, often based on coconut milk, tend to be colourful and sweet. Alternatively, you can choose from the wide variety of succulent fresh fruits. Meals are normally consumed with spoon and fork, although noodles demand chopsticks.

Northern dishes, with Burmese influence, are less fiery and tend towards meats, whereas the southern coasts offer grilled lobster, crab and tiger prawns. Try *nam-prik ong*, a chilli dip served with pork crackling and cooked vegetables, or *khai pad jihn-som*, made with sliced sausage, scrambled eggs, garlic and herbs. The best-known dish of the north-east is *som tam*. This is green papaya salad with dried shrimp, lime juice, garlic and chillies. The central region offers an eclectic selection, including such soups as *tom yam kung* (spicy lemon soup with prawns) or *tom kha ghai* (chicken soup with coconut). Fast food includes *phat thai* (noodles with prawns), *khao phat* (fried rice with a choice of chopped pork, chicken, prawns and egg) and *phat kha pao* (steamed rice with a choice of meats or seafood, basil, chilli and a fried egg on top). Look also for *moo chóup pang tod* (pork with pineapple, ginger, garlic and vegetables), *gai yang sauce ma-muang* (chicken with lemon grass, orange, garlic, ginger and ripe mango) and *khao ob sapalot* (chopped ham, raisins, garlic, onion, ginger, bell pepper cooked in a pineapple). A similar southern dish, *gaeng khai mang-da*, combines horseshoe crab eggs with pineapple curry.

Above: The rich diversity of colour and flavours is apparent in the selection of dishes displayed.

Green curry is popular (*kaeng keow wan*) using various meats or seafood. Also try red curry (*kaeng ped*), yellow, *penang* or *masaman*. All include coconut milk and are as spicy as you prefer. Noodles, white or yellow, make soup (*kwiteo nam*) or are fried (*kwiteo hehng*) with vegetables. Also enjoy ripe mango with sticky rice and coconut milk.

6 *Loch Palm*

Loch Palm Golf Club, 38 Moo 5, Vichitsongkram Road, Kathu District, Phuket 83120
TEL: *(076) 321 930* **FAX:** *(076) 321 927-8*
LOCATION: *7km west of Phuket town near Kathu, access via Route 4020*
COURSE: *18 holes, 6561yd/5999m, par 72*
TYPE OF COURSE: *Gently undulating parkland around two large lakes*
DESIGNER: *Dr Sukitti Klangvisai (1994)*
GREEN FEES: *BBBBB*
FACILITIES: *Golf shop, caddies, cart and golf equipment hire, shoe and chair and umbrella rental, driving range, putting green, changing facilities, refreshment shelters on course, restaurant in clubhouse*
VISITORS: *Welcome, but advance reservation necessary. Soft spikes and dress code*

With an evocative change of name and the opening of a substantial clubhouse, this course is making a determined effort to stand up and be counted. A further 1400 palm trees have been added to the layout, which runs over mildly undulating land, circumnavigating two lakes and ringed by a comforting cloak of wooded hills. The larger of these, Crystal Lake, is a serious factor on the opening three holes and water can prove a slicer's nightmare on the first seven. The course is not too long but punishments can be severe; the view, however, is peaceful and relaxing. The club is currently the only one on Phuket island to have golf carts; its driving range also offers the novelty of hitting floating balls into water, under the gaze of clubhouse terrace diners who can enjoy a scenic lakeside view.

This is relaxed, not too intimidating golf, but highly priced by Thai standards. Only eight courses in this book have a published green fee at this level or higher; somewhat surprisingly, six of them are in the Phuket area.

There are a number of attractive lodges on the course available for rent and, in the pleasant, well-equipped clubhouse, there is a herbal sauna and Thai massage. Laid out in a peaceful, away-from-it-all setting, Loch Palm has much to offer.

Below: With Crystal Lake below on the right, the 529-yd/484-m 18th hole doglegs left around a rocky outcrop – a highly strategic finish.

Fruitful Delights

One of the memorable pleasures experienced by visitors to Thailand is the wealth and great variety of domestic fruit. Blessed with a warm, tropical climate and sufficient variation between the deep south and far mountainous north, there is a rich and delicious choice to be made every month of the year. What is more, many are varieties of fruit not normally seen in cooler countries, exotic and colourful, sweet or tangy, a tropical bounty worth the experience. In addition, the ever-resourceful Thais can turn some fruit and some humble vegetables into works of art. The centrepiece in many buffet tables, even a corner of your plate, can be a wonderfully surreal display of delicate flowers, perhaps orchids or roses, and birds, all skilfully carved by experienced hands from carrot, tomato, white radish or watermelon. A delicious feast for the eye as well as the table.

While some fruits are seasonal, many are available all year round, and you can expect to enjoy them wherever you happen to be staying. A number of fruits grown in Thailand will be instantly recognizable to the international market. Strawberries, lemon, lime and oranges, the latter more closely resembling tangerines in appearance, are readily available as are bananas and both black and white grapes. Pineapples tend to be larger and much sweeter than most found abroad, particularly the 'honey' variety that is found in the north. In fact, some Thais even eat pineapples sprinkled with salt. Mangos can be eaten green or, better still, at the time when they are sweetly ripe and deliciously served with sticky rice and coconut milk, a Northern favourite. You can also enjoy cantaloupe and large, juicy, refreshing watermelons.

More exotic is the large, spiky durian, noted for its pungent smell. Other large fleshy fruit include papaya and jackfruit, plus pomelo – built like a large, mild grapefruit. Northerners look forward to May and the time for lychee, lum yai and longan, each concealing delicate white flesh. One month later is the time for mangosteen and juicy, fuzzy rambutan. Look out also for mimusops, rose apple, zalacca and spicy tamarind. Young coconuts, picked fresh off the tree by trained monkeys, provide both beverage and tender meat. Coconut cream is also a key ingredient of many Thai curries, while ice cream made with this indigenous and versatile fruit is an exotic experience. The greatest variety of fruits come from the east and south of the country, while vegetables are grown more in the north. To Thai people, presentation is a key ingredient to any food and even simple platters of sliced fruit will have been lovingly carved and shaped.

Above: The delicate art of fruit and vegetable carving originated in the Royal household.

REGIONAL DIRECTORY

Where to stay
Phuket

Dusit Laguna (076 324 320-32, Fax: 076 324 174) On a narrow isthmus at the centre of Laguna resort, this exclusive hotel in a tropical garden setting has water on two sides and the clear 3-km/2-mile stretch of white-sand beach on the other. The relaxed ambience coupled with immaculate service that is a Dusit byword is best described as 'barefoot luxury'. The 226 tastefully decorated rooms and suites fan out from the centre under scented flowering trees and palms with views of the shimmering sea. Diners can choose from Royal Thai cuisine in the teak splendour of Ruenthai, Italian specialities at La Trattoria, fresh seafood on the beach at Casurina Hut in high season or the all-day selection in the Laguna Café. There are two swimming pools plus a whirlpool, floodlit tennis, three holes of pitch and putt, table tennis, volleyball and a full range of watersports.

Laguna Beach Resort (076 324 352, Fax: 076 324 353) Just a casual ferry trip across the lagoon from the Dusit, this popular low-rise hotel in traditional Thai style offers attractive balcony views from its 252 rooms and 34 suites. In tastefully landscaped grounds, guests can enjoy a full range of activities, including the four-acre water park with expert tuition, tennis, squash, archery or just lazing in the pool. Five restaurants offer Thai, Asian and Continental specialities as well as fresh seafood. Meals are often accompanied by live music and cultural shows. Inter-hotel dining transfers apply.

Blue Canyon Country Club (076 327 440-7, Fax: 076 327 449) Golf addicts may prefer to stay overlooking the pristine 36 holes of the Blue Canyon courses. This offers a setting of peaceful isolation with lakes, mature trees and the layout where Tiger Woods won the 1998 Johnnie Walker Classic. The Golfers' Lodge, spreading high across the rocky promontory above the clubhouse level and the Canyon itself, has 49 spacious well-furnished rooms, all with exceptional balcony views. Dining choice is between the Canyon Restaurant, which serves Thai, European or Japanese fare, or the open-air relaxation of the Golfers' Terrace in the Clubhouse below. In addition to the excellent golf, there is a swimming pool, tennis courts, sauna, whirlpool, fitness room and massage. There are complimentary transfers to the nearby airport and yacht charters.

Hat Yai

Central Sukhontha Hotel (074 352 222, Fax: 074 352 223) Rising above the Central Department Store in downtown Hat Yai, this modern hotel is ideally placed for shopping, with the Santisuk Market also close by. In addition to all-day dining in the Saneha Café, the Southern Palace serves traditional Chinese cuisine plus dim sum. As you would expect for a hotel favoured by business travellers and for conventions, facilities and service – both in the 238 rooms and throughout the hotel – are comprehensive. These include a swimming pool, fitness centre and sauna.

Where to Eat
Phuket

The primary attraction in Phuket is the fresh seafood, especially lobster. There are many hotels, each with a selection of attractive restaurants, often in idyllic seaview settings. There are also a vast array of outside alternatives, ranging from the exclusive to more popular, mostly along the western beaches of Karon, Kata, Surin, Patong and Chalong Bay. The choice ranges from Dutch, English, French, German, Italian, Indian, Japanese, Mexican, Mongolian, Scandinavian, Swiss, Thai and American. All the world is here, especially in the polyglot selection that is Patong Beach, but treasures can be found. **Baan Rim Pa** (076 340 789) perched on a cliff overlooking Patong Bay offers superb Thai food in a romantic setting. **The Boathouse Wine and Grill** (076 330 015) is on Kata Beach, with a well-deserved reputation for its wine cellar as well as Thai, European and seafood dishes. Unpretentious but in demand, **Kan Eang Seafood** (076 381 212 or 381 323) serves the day's catch, lobsters, oysters and the rich harvest of the sea under trees along the edge of Chalong Bay.

Hat Yai

For steaks, Italian or Thai food with live music, try **Toscana** (074 342 429). Try **Jao Seafood Restaurant** (074 237 501) for Chinese or **Pho Vietnamese** (074 357 831) for authentic flavours.

What to See
Phuket

Phuket's history reflects the cultural mix of European, Chinese and Malaysian influence. This can be seen in many buildings in the Old Town and various temples and mosques. **Wat Phra Thong** is famous for its partially buried golden Buddha. A day trip by boat to **Phang Nga Bay** reveals the large number of fascinating uninhabited limestone outcrops, including Kao Tapoo, sometimes called 'James Bond Island' (see p.141), and Muslim fishing villages on stilts over the sea.

Hat Yai

Check out local culture such as Manohra dancers and Nang Talung shadow plays. The Central Mosque at **Pattani** is Thailand's largest and arguably most beautiful.

Other Courses in Thailand

BANGKOK AND CENTRAL PLAINS
Bangpoo Country Club
Tel: (02) 324 0320-9 Fax: (02) 324 0330
18 holes, 7141yd/6530m, par 72

Kiartee Thanee Country Club
Tel: (02) 707 1700-9 Fax: (02) 707 1710
18 holes, 6730yd/6154m, par 72

Krung Kavee Golf & Country Club
Tel: (02) 577 2891-4 Fax: (02) 577 2894
18 holes, 7082yd/6476m, par 72

Krungthep Kreetha Sports Club
Tel: (02) 379 3716 Fax: (02) 379 3768
18 holes, 6874yd/6285m, par 72

Muang Ake Golf Course
Tel: (02) 533 9335-40 Fax: (02) 533 9345
18 holes, 6398yd/5850m, par 72

Muang Ake Wang-Noi Golf Club
Tel: (035) 214 825-9 Fax: (035) 214 828
18 holes, 6830yd/6245m, par 72

Natural Park Ramindra Golf Club
Tel: (02) 914 1930-60 Fax: 914 1970-1
18 holes, 6984yd/6386m, par 72

Northern Rangsit Golf Club
Tel: (035) 271 755-6 Fax: (035) 215 413
18 holes, 6782yd/6201m, par 72

Panya Indra Golf Club
Tel: (02) 519 5840-4 Fax: (02) 519 5843
27 holes, 3652yd/3339m, 3608yd/3299m,
3501yd/3201m, all par 36

Pinehurst Golf & Golf Club
Tel: (02) 516 8679-84 Fax: (02) 516 8685
27 holes, 3453yd/3157m, 3402yd/3111m,
3398yd/3107m, all par 36

Royal Thai Army Sports Centre
Tel: (02) 521 5338-9 Fax: (02) 521 3391
36 holes, 6924yd/6331m, par 72, 6206yd/5674m,
par 71

Royal Thai Air Force Kantarat Golf Club
Tel: (02) 534 3840 Fax: (02) 523 6441
18 holes, 6449yd/5897m, par 72

Uniland Golf & Country Club
Tel: (034) 271 351-3 Fax: (034) 271 351-3
18 holes, 6982yd/6384m, par 72

The Vintage Club
Tel: (02) 707 3820-7 Fax: (02) 707 3829
18 holes, 6579yd/6015m, par 72

Windmill Park Country Club
Tel: (02) 316 9591-2 Fax: (02) 316 8268
18 holes, 6956yd/6360m, par 72

EASTERN SEABOARD
Chonburi Century Country Club
Tel: (01) 304 1545 Fax: (038) 443 837
18 holes, 6991yd/6392m, par 72

Great Lake Golf & Country Club
Tel: (038) 622 630 Fax: (038) 622 630
18 holes, 6934yd/6340m, par 72

Rayong Century Golf & Country Club
Tel: (038) 602 889 Fax: (038) 602 889
18 holes, 6554yd/5992m, par 72

Sriracha International Golf Club
Tel: (038) 338 375-8 Fax: (038) 338 379
18 holes, 7019yd/6418m, par 72

NORTHERN REGION
Gymkhana Club Golf Course
Tel: (053) 241 035 Fax: (053) 247 352
9 holes, 2953yd/2700m, par 36

WESTERN REGION
Bangkok Golf Milford & Resort
Tel: (032) 572 441 Fax: (032) 572 440
18 holes, 6614yd/6047m, par 72

SOUTHERN REGION
Banyan Tree Phuket Golf Club
Tel: (076) 324 350 Fax: (076) 324 351
18 holes, 6768yd/6188m, par 71

Additional Information

GETTING BY IN THAI

Most hotels, golf clubs and other facilities dealing with tourists can speak English as well as Thai, sometimes also French. Elsewhere, a few words of Thai may prove helpful. Note that Thais put the adjective after the noun, not before, as in 'taxi meter' or 'bar beer'

1 *neung*	**5** *ha*	**9** *gao*	**20** *yi-sip*
2 *song*	**6** *hok*	**10** *sam*	**21** *yi-sip-et*
3 *sam*	**7** *jet*	**11** *sip-et*	
4 *si*	**8** *paed*	**12** *sip-song*	

Sunday *wan-athit*
Monday *wan-jan*
Tuesday *wan-angkaan*
Wednesday *wan-phut*
Thursday *wan-paruehat-sa-bo-di*
Friday *wan-suk*
Saturday *wan-sao*

today *wan-ni*		**hour** *chua-mong*
tonight *kuen-ni*		**day** *wan*
tomorrow *proong-ni*		**week** *sub-da*
yesterday *muea-waan-ni*		**month** *duean*
second *wi-na-tee*		**year** *pee*
minute *na-tee*		

Good morning *sa-wad-di* (also good afternoon, good evening, good night, hello, goodbye)
Mr/Mrs/Miss *khun*
yes *chai*
no *mai*
thank you *khop-khun*
how are you? *khun-sa-bai-di-ru*
very well, thank you *sa-bai-di, khop-khun*
excuse me *kho-thot*
very good *di-mak*
How much do you want? *khun-tong-kan-thao-rai*
Too expensive *paeng-pai*
Any discount? *lot-ra-kha-noi-dai-mai*
Can you help me? *chuay-noi-dai-mai*
Where is...? *...yuu-ti-nai?*
Where is the lavatory? *hong-na-yu-ti-nai?*
Please drive slowly *prot-put-cha-cha*
Do you speak English? *khun-pood-pa-sa-angrid-dai-mai?*
I don't understand *chan-mai-khao-jai*
Thanks for your help *khop-khon-ti-chuay*
bank *ta-na-kam*
exchange rate *at-tra-laeg-ngern*
credit card *bat-credit*
tailor shop *raan-tad-suea*

gold shop *raan tong*
jewellery store *raan-kaai-pet-ploy*
go *pai*
stop *yud*
wait *raw-koi*

TOUR OPERATORS

There are a number of overseas tour operators offering complete holidays with golf for both individuals and groups. There are also specialist ground handlers who can arrange golf and transportation within the Kingdom.

From Europe
Silverbird Travel (General UK sales agent for Royal Orchid Holidays) Tel: (020) 8875 9191; Fax: (020) 8875 1874 e-mail: sales@silverbird.co.uk
Coco Golf (Eastern Seaboard, Kanchanaburi and the North) Tel: (01959) 532 243 (UK); Fax: (01959) 533 830 (UK); www.cocogolf.co.uk
Asean Explorer (Eastern Seaboard and the North) Tel: (01481) 823 417 (UK); Fax:(01481) 823 495 (UK); e-mail: info@asean-explorer.com
Distant Landings (All main golfing regions) Tel: (023) 8058 2004 (UK); Fax: (023) 8058 2013 (UK); e-mail: distant.landings@virgin.net
Chaka Travel (Most golfing regions) Tel: (028) 9020 3010 Fax: (028) 9020 3033 (UK); e-mail: mark@chakatravel.com

In Thailand
World Splendour Holidays (Most golfing regions) Tel: (02) 271 2559; Fax: (02) 271 0616; e-mail: wshs@samart.co.th
Coco Golf (Eastern Seaboard, Kanchanaburi and the North) Tel: (038) 429 609; Fax: (038) 423 880; www.cocogolf.co.uk
Thailand Tee-Off Service (Northern specialist; also regional offers) Tel: (053) 260 612; Fax: (053) 398 908; e-mail: magnus@ cm.ksc.co.th
Hua Hin Golf Tours (Western region specialist plus Kanchanaburi) Tel: (032) 530 119; Fax: (032) 512 085; e-mail: hhgolf@huahingolf.com
P.G.Golf (Phuket specialist) Tel/Fax: (076) 381 064

Thai Tourist Offices

HEAD OFFICE
Le Concorde Building, 202
Rathchadaphisek Road, Huai
Khwang, Bangkok 10310,
Thailand
Tel: (66 2) 694 1222 (80 lines)
Fax: (66 2) 694 1220-1
www.tat.or.th or
www.tourismthailand.org
E-mail: center@tat.or.th

LOCAL OFFICES

North
TAT Northern Office: Region 1
105/1 Chiang Mai-Lamphun
Road, Amphoe Muang, Chiang
Mai 50000
Tel: (66 53) 248 604, 248 607,
241 466
Fax: (66 53) 248 605
E-mail: tatcnx@samart.co.th
Areas of responsibility: Chiang
Mai, Lamphun, Lampang and Mae
Hong Son

TAT Northern Office: Region 2
448/16 Singhachau Road,
Amphoe Muang, Chiang Rai
57000
Tel: (66 53) 717 433, 744 674-5
Fax: (66 53) 717 434
E-mail: tatcei@loxinfo.co.th
Areas of responsibility: Chiang
Rai, Phayao, Phrae and Nan

TAT Northern Office: Region 3
209/7-8 Surasi Trade Center,
Boromtrailokanat Road, Amphoe
Muang, Phitsanulok 65000
Tel: (66 55) 252 743, 259 907
Fax: (66 55) 252 742
E-mail: tatphs@loxinfo.co.th
Areas of responsibility:
Phitsanulok, Phetchabun, Sukothai
and Uttaradit

TAT Northern Office: Region 4
193 Taksin Road, Tambon
Nong Luang, Amphoe Muang,
Tak 63000
Tel: (66 55) 514 341/3
Fax: (66 55) 514 344
E-mail: tattak@north.shane.net
Areas of responsibility: Tak, Phichi
and Kamphaeng Phet

Central
TAT Central Office: Region 1
Saeng Chuto Road, Amphoe
Muang, Kanchanaburi 71000
Tel: (66 34) 511 200, 512 500
Fax: (66 34) 511 200
Areas of responsibility:
Kanchanaburi, Nakhon Pathom,
Samut Sakhon and Samut
Songkhram

TAT Central Office: Region 2
500/51 Phetkasem Road, Amphoe
Cha-am, Phetchaburi 76120
Tel: (66 32) 471 005, 471 502
Fax: (66 32) 471 502
E-mail: tatphet@tat.or.th
Areas of responsibility: Phetchaburi
(Cha-Am), Ratchaburi and
Prachuap Khiri Khan

TAT Central Office: Region 3
609 Moo 10, Phra Tham Nak
Road, Tambon Nongpue,
Amphoe Bang Lamung,
Chonburi 20260
Tel: (66 38) 427 667, 428 750
Fax: (66 38) 429 113
E-mail: tatpty@chonburi.ksc.co.th
Areas of responsibility: Chonburi
(Pattaya)

TAT Central Office: Region 4
153/4 Sukhumvit Road, Amphoe
Muang, Rayong 21000
Tel: (66 38) 655 420-1, 664 585
Fax: (66 38) 655 422
E-mail: tatry@infonews.co.th
Areas of responsibility: Rayong and
Chanthaburi

TAT Central Office: Region 5
100 Moo 1, Trat–Laemngob
Road, Tambon Laemngob,
Amphoe Laemngob, Trat 23120
Tel: (66 39) 597 255, 597 259-60
Fax: (66 39) 597 255
Areas of responsibility: Trat and its
islands

TAT Central Office: Region 6
108/22 Moo 4, Amphoe Phra,
Nakhon Si Ayutthaya, Phra
Kakhon Si Ayutthaya 13000

Tel: (66 35) 246 076-7
Fax: (66 35) 246 078
Areas of responsibility: Phra
Nakhon Si Ayutthaya, Saraburi,
Ang Thong, Suphan Buri, Pathum
Thani and Nonthaburi

TAT Central Office: Region 7
Rop Wat Phratat Road, Muang
District, Lop Buri 15000
Tel: (66 36) 422 768-9
Fax: (66 36) 424 089
Areas of responsibility: Lop Buri,
Nakhon Sawan, Uthai Thani, Chai
Nat and Sing Buri

TAT Central Office: Region 8
182/88 Moo 1, Suwannason
Road, Tambon Thachang,
Amphoe Muang, Nakhon
Nayok 26000
Tel: (66 37) 312 282, 312 284
Fax: (66 37) 312 286
E-mail: tatnayok@tat.or.th
Areas of responsibility: Nakhon
Nayok, Sa Kaeo, Prachin Buri and
Chachoengsao

Northeast
TAT Northeastern Office: Region
1, 2102-2104 Mittraphap Road,
Tambon Nai Muang, Amphoe
Muang, Nakhon Ratchasima
30000
Tel: (66 44) 213 666, 213 030
Fax: (66 44) 213 667
Areas of responsibility: Nakhon
Ratchasima, Buri Ram, Surin and
Chaiyaphum

TAT Northeastern Office: Region
2, 264/1 Khaun Thani Road,
Amphoe Muang, Ubon
Ratchathani 34000
Tel: (66 45) 243 770-1
Fax: (66 45) 243 771
Areas of responsibility: Ubon
Ratchathani, Amnat Charoen, Si
Sa Ket and Yasothon

TAT Northeastern Office: Region
3, 15/5 Prachasamosorn Road,
Amphoe Muang, Khon Kaen
40000
Tel: (66 43) 244 498-9
Fax: (66 43) 244 497

Areas of responsibility: Khon Kaen, Roi Et, Maha Sarakham and Kalasin

TAT Northeastern Office: Region 4, 184/1 Soontornvijit Road, Tambon Nai Muang, Amphoe Muang, Nakhon Phanom 48000
Tel: (66 42) 513 490-1
Fax: (66 42) 513 492
E-mail: tat.ne@npu.msu.ac.th
Areas of responsibility: Nakhon Phanom, Sakhon Nakhon and Mukdahan

TAT Northeastern Office: Region 5
16/5 Muk Montri Road, Muang District, Udon Thani 41000
Tel: (66 42) 325 406-7
Mobile: (66 1) 462 2112
Fax: (66 42) 325 408
Areas of responsibility: Udon Thani, Nong Bua Lamphu, Nong Khai and Loei

South
TAT Southern Office: Region 1
1/1 Soi 2, Niphat Uthit 3 Road, Hat Yai District, Songkhla 90110
Tel (66 74) 231 055, 238 518
Mobile: (66 1) 478 8493
Fax: (66 74) 245 986
E-mail: tathatyai@hatyai.inet.co.th
Areas of responsibility: Songkhla (Hat Yai) and Satun

TAT Southern Office: Region 2
Sanam Na Muang Ratchadamnoen Road, Muang District, Nakhon Si Thammarat 80000
Tel: (66 75) 346 515-6
Mobile: (66 1) 979 1242
Fax: (66 75) 346517
Areas of responsibility: Nakhon Si Thammarat, Trang and Phattalung

TAT Southern Office: Region 3
102/3 Moo 2, Muang District, Narathiwat 96120
Tel: (66 73) 516 144
Mobile: (66 1) 957 5647
Fax: (66 73) 516 144
E-mail: tatnara@cscoms.com
Areas of responsibility: Narathiwat, Yala and Pattani

TAT Southern Office: Region 4
73–75 Phuket Road, Muang District, Phuket 83000
Tel: (66 76) 211 036, 212 213

Mobile: (66 1) 476 2848
Fax: (66 76) 213 582
E-mail: tathkt@phuket.ksc.co.th
Areas of responsibility: Phuket, Phang Nga and Krabi

TAT Southern Office: Region 5
5 Talad Mai Road, Ban Don, Muang District, Surat Thani 84000
Tel: (66 77) 288 818-9, 281 828
Mobile: (66 1) 476 6115
Fax: (66 77) 282 828
E-mail: tatsurat@samart.co.th
Areas of responsibility:Surat Thani, Chumphon and Ranong

OVERSEAS OFFICES

Asia & Pacific

Kuala Lumpur
Tourism Authority of Thailand
Suite 22.01, Level 22, Menera Lion, 165 Jalan Ampang, 50450 Kuala Lumpur, Malaysia
Tel: (007 60 3) 262 3480
Fax: (007 60 3) 262 3486
E-mail: sawatdi@po.jaring.my
Areas of responsibility: Malaysia and Brunei

Singapore
Tourism Authority of Thailand
c/o Royal Thai Embassy, 370 Orchard Road, Singapore 238870
Tel: (65) 235 7694, 235 7901
Fax: (65) 733 5653
E-mail: atsin@mbox5.singnet.com.sg
Areas of responsibility: Singapore, Indonesia and The Philippines

Hong Kong
Tourism Authority of Thailand
401 Fairmont House, 8 Cotton Tree Drive, Central Hong Kong
Tel: (85 2) 2868 0732, 2868 0854
Fax: (85 2) 2868 4585
E-mail: tathkg@hk.super.net
Areas of responsibility: Hong Kong, Macau and People's Republic of China

Taipei
Thailand Tourism Division
13 Floor, Boss Tower, No 111 Sung Chiang Road, (Near Nanking East Road Junction), Taipei 104, Taiwan
Tel: (886 2) 2502 1600

Fax: (886 2) 2502 1603
E-mail: tattpe@ms3.hinet.net
Area of responsibility: Taiwan

Seoul
Tourism Authority of Thailand
Coryo Daeyungak Center Building, RM. No. 604, 6th Fl., 25-5, 1-Ka, Chungmu-Ro, Chung-Ku, Seoul 100-706, Korea
Tel: (82 2) 779 5417, 779 5418, 771 9650
Fax: (82 2) 779 5419
E-mail: tatsel@soback.kornet.nm.kr
Area of responsibility: Republic of Korea

Tokyo
Tourism Authority of Thailand
Yurakucho Denki Building, South Tower 2F, Room No. 259, 1-7-1 Yurakucho, Chiyoda-ku, Tokyo 100, Japan
Tel: (81 3) 3218 0337, 3218 0355, 3218 1077
Fax: (81 3) 3218 0655
E-mail: tattky@crisscross.com
Areas of responsibility: Northern Area of Honshu Island, Tohoku, Kanto and Hokkaido Island

Osaka
Tourism Authority of Thailand
Technoble Yotsubashi Building 3F, 1-6-8 Kitahorie, Nishi-ku, Osaka 550-0014, Japan
Tel: (81 6) 6543 6654, 6543 6655
Fax: (81 6) 6543 6660
E-mail: tatosa@ca.mbn.or.jp
Areas of responsibility: Southern Area of Honshu Island, Kinki, Chugoku and Chubu

Fukuoka
Tourism Authority of Thailand
El Gala Bldg. 6F, 1-4-2 Tenjin, Chuo-ku, Fukuoka 810-0001, Japan
Tel: (81 92) 725 8808
Fax: (81 92) 735 4434
E-mail: tatfuk@asahi-net.or.jp
Areas of responsibility: Kyushu Island, Shikoku Island and Okinawa

Sydney
Tourism Authority of Thailand
2nd Floor, 75 Pitt Street, Sydney, NSW 2000, Australia
Tel: (61 2) 9247 7549
Fax: (61 2) 9251 2465
E-mail: info@thailand.net.au

Areas of responsibility: Australia, New Zealand and South Pacific

Europe

Frankfurt
Thailandisches
Fremdenverkehrsamt
Bethmannstr. 58 D-60311,
Frankfurt/M
Tel: (49 69) 1381 390
Fax: (49 69) 281 468
E-mail: tatfra@t-online.de
Areas of responsibility: Germany, Austria, Switzerland and Eastern Europe

London
Tourism Authority of Thailand
49 Albemarle Street, London
W1X 3FE
Tel: (44 20) 7499 7679
Fax: (44 20) 7629 5519
E-mail: info@tat-uk.demon.co.uk
Areas of responsibility: United Kingdom, Ireland, Finland and Scandinavia

Paris
Office National du Tourisme
Thailandais
90 Avenue des Champs Elysees,
75008 Paris
Tel: (33 1) 5353 4700 (10 lines)
Fax: (33 1) 4563 7888

E-mail: tatpar@wanadoo.fr
Areas of responsibility: France, Belgium, Luxembourg and the Netherlands

Rome
Ente Nazionale per il Turismo
Thailandese
Via Barberini, 68, 4th Floor,
00187 Roma
Tel: (39 06) 487 3497, 481 8927
Fax: (39 06) 487 3500
E-mail: tat.rome@iol.it
Areas of responsibility: Italy, Spain, Greece, Portugal, Israel, Egypt and Turkey

USA

Los Angeles
Tourism Authority of Thailand
611 North Larchmont Boulevard,
1st Flr, Los Angeles, CA 90004
Tel: (1 323) 461 9814
Fax: (1 323) 461 9834
E-mail: tatla@ix.netcom.com
Areas of responsibility: Alaska, Arizona, California, Colorado, Hawaii, Idaho, Kansas, Montana, Nebraska, Nevada, New Mexico, North Dakota, Oklahoma, Oregon, South Dakota, Texas, Utah, Washington, Wyoming, Guam Island and all Central and Southern American Countries, all

West Canada: Alberta, British Columbia, Manitoba, Northwest-Territories, Saskatchewan and Yukon

New York
Tourism Authority of Thailand
c/o Royal Thai Consulate-General, 351 East 52nd Street,
New York, N.Y. 10022
Tel: (1 212) 754 2536-8, 754 1770
Fax: (1 212) 754 1907
E-mail: thainycg@aol.com
Areas of responsibility: Alabama, Arkansas, Connecticut, Delaware, Florida, Georgia, Illinois, Indiana, Iowa, Kentucky, Louisiana, Maine, Maryland, Massachusetts, Michigan, Minnesota, Mississippi, Missouri, New York, New Hampshire, North Carolina, Ohio, South Carolina, Tennessee, Vermont, Virginia, West Virginia, Wisconsin, Puerto Rico and the Bahamas, all East Canada: Ontario, Quebec, New Brunswick, Nova Scotia and Newfoundland

Index

18 holes, the best 18–21
accommodation 14
air travel 12–13

Bangkapong Riverside 49
Bangkok
   area 22–53
   city 23–5
   Golf Club 32–3
   Milford & Resort 154
Bangpoo Country Club 154
Bangpra 8, 18, 64–5
Bangsai Country Club 18, 19,
   34–5
Banyan Tree Phuket Golf Club
   154
beaches 140
best 18 holes 18–21
Blue Canyon
   (Canyon) 20, 21, 144–5
   (Lakes) 146
Buddhism 85, 120
buses 14
business hours 16

caddies 78
canals 23
car travel 13
cemeteries, World War II 111
central plains 22–53
championship courses
   Blue Canyon 144–5
   Mission Hills 86–7
   Natural Park Hill 58–9
   Navatanee 40–1
   Springfield Royal 128–9
   Thai
      Country Club 46–7
      Muang Beach 142–3
Chatuchak market 25
Chiang Rai 94
Chiangmai
   Green Valley 100
   Lamphun 20, 98–9
Chonburi Century Country Club
   154
crafts 15, 16
culture 9, 93, 106, 139–40
currency 15
customs 10–12

desert courses
   Imperial Lake View 126–7
   Khao-Yai Country Club 88
design, golf courses 136
Don Muang airport course 90
Dragon Hills 19, 112–13

drinks 14–15
Dusit 51
Dye Design Inc 142
Dye, Perry O. 148
Dynasty 19, 28–9

Eastern
   seaboard 54–79
   Star 74–5
elephants 94
Engh, Jim 112
etiquette 16–17, 62
Evergreen Hills 116–17

festivals 120
food 14–15, 150, 152
Forest Hills 84–5
Fream, Ronald 42, 58
Friendship Meadows 89
fruit 152

Grand Palace 24
Great Lake Golf & Country Club
   154
Green Valley 37
Griffiths, Dennis 29, 46, 71, 76
Gymkhana Club Golf Course 154

Hat Yai 141
health 12, 17
heathland courses
   Noble Place 62–3
   Thana City 36
Hilltribe People 106
history 50–51, 136
holidays 17
horse racing 50
hotels 52–3, 79, 91, 107, 121, 137,
   153
Hua Hin 123

Imperial Lake View 126–7
insurance 10
island resorts 56–7, 139
Izumi, I. 70

Kato, Yoshikazu 144
Khao Kheow 61
Khao-Yai Country Club 88
Khmer temples 83
Kiartee Thanee Country Club 154
Krung Kavee Golf & Country
   Club 154
Krungthep Kreetha Sports Club
   154

Laem Chabang 18, 66–7

Lakes see Blue Canyon (Lakes)
Lam Luk Ka 38–9
Lanna
   kingdom 93
   Sports Centre 101
links courses
   Bangsai Country Club 34–5
   Noble Place 62–3
   Royal Chiangmai 96–7
   Thana City 36
location of courses 10, 11
Loch Palm 151
Loy Krathong 120

Majestic Creek, The 20, 130–31
maps
   Bankok area 23
   Eastern seaboard 56
   Northern region 95
   Saraburi region 83
   Southern region 141
   Thailand 11
   Western
      Kanchanaburi 110
      region 124
Mission Hills
   Kanchanaburi 114–15
   Saraburi 86–7
Mon kingdom 109
mountain courses
   Forest Hills 84–5
   Laem Chabang 66–7
   Mission Hills 86–7
   Nichigo Resort 118–19
   Royal
      Hua Hin 132–3
      Ratchaburi 26
   Soi Dao Highland 76–7
movies 141
Muang Ake
   Golf Course 154
   Wang-Noi Golf Club 154

National Parks 82
Natural Park
   Hill 18, 58–9
   Ramindra Golf Club 154
   Resort 60, 60
Navatanee 19, 40–41
Nichigo Resort 118–19
Nicklaus, Jack 86, 88, 114, 128
nightlife 25
Noble Place 20, 62–3
Norman, Greg 36
Northern
   Rangsit Golf Club 154
   region 92–107

Packard, Roger 38–9, 126
Palm Hills 134
Panya
  Indra Golf Club 154
  Park 42–3
parkland courses
  Bangkapong Riverside 49
  Bangpra 64–5
  Blue Canyon 144–5
  Chiangmai-Lamphun 98–9
  Dragon Hills 112–13
  Evergreen Hills 116–17
  Forest Hills 84–5
  Friendship Meadows 89
  Green Valley 37
  Lam Luk Ka 38–9
  Lanna Sports Centre 101
  Loch Palm 151
  Mission Hills Kanchanaburi
    114–15
  Navatanee 40–41
  Nichigo Resort 118–19
  Palm Hills 134
  Panya Park 42–3
  Phoenix 71
  Phuket Country Club 147
  President Country Club 44–5
  Rayong Green Valley 72–3
  Rose Garden, The 30–31
  Royal
    Chiangmai 96–7
    Hua Hin 132–3
    Ratchaburi 26
  Santiburi Country Club 102–3
  Sawang Resort 135
  Siam Country Club 70
  Soi Dao Highland 76–7
  Subhapruek 48
  Treasure Hill 68
  Waterford Valley 104–5
Pattaya 55–6
  Country Club 69
Phang Nga Bay 138, 141
Phoenix 71
Phra Buddha Chinaraj 14
Phuket 139–40
  Country Club 147
Pinehurst Golf Club 154
playing season 10
Prasat Phra Thep Bidom 22
President Country Club 44–5

railways 14, 111, 125
Rayong
  Century Golf & Country Club
    154
  Green Valley 72–3
resort courses
  Bangkok Golf Club 33
  Bangpra 64–5
  Forest Hills 84–5

Imperial Lake View 126–7
  Laem Chabang 66–7
  Mission Hills 86–7
  Natural Park
    Hill 58–9
    Resort 60
  Nichigo Resort 118–19
  Palm Hills 134
  Rose Garden, The 30–31
  Royal Chiangmai 96–7
  Sawang Resort 135
  Southern Hills 148–9
  Thai Muang Beach 142–3
  Waterford Valley 104–5
resorts 51, 55, 57, 81, 109, 123
restaurants 53, 79, 91, 107, 121,
  137, 153
River Kwai 111
Robins, A. O. 132
Rose Garden, The 20, 30–31
Royal
  Chiangmai 21, 96–7
  history 123, 125
  Hua Hin 51, 123, 132–3
  Ratchaburi 9, 21, 26–7
  rituals 115
  ThaiAir Force Kantarat Golf
    Club 154

sand hazards
  Eastern Star 74–5
  Panya Park 42–3
  Springfield Royal 128
  Thai Country Club 46–7
Santiburi 21
  Country Club 102–3
Saraburi region 80–91
Sawang Resort 135
self-drive 13–14
Siam Country Club 70
Siamese sports 29
Soi Dao Highland 19, 56, 76–7
Songkhla 141
Southern
  Hills 148–9
  region 138–53
Spirit Houses 94
Springfield Royal 20, 128–9
Sriracha International Golf Club
  154
Subhapruek 48
Sukhum Sukapanpotharam 98
Sukitti Klangvisai 130

temples 24, 83, 93–4
Thai
  Airways International 12, 13
  Boxing 57
  Country Club 46–7
  Muang Beach 21, 21, 142–3
Thana City 36

Thomson and Wolveridge 62, 72
Thonburi 24
tipping 15–16
tour operators 155
tourist offices 156–8
travel 10–14, 73
Treasure Hill 68
Trent Jones, Robert Jr 37, 40, 44,
  74, 102
tropical golf tips 117

Uniland Golf & Country Club 154
unusual courses 90

valley courses
  Bangpra 64–5
  Chiangmai-Lamphun 98–9
  Dragon Hills 112–13
  Khao Kheow 61
  Laem Chabang 66–7
  Rayong Green Valley 72–3
  Southern Hills 148–9
  Waterford Valley 104–5
Vintage Club, The 154
Visudh Junnanont 30

wai greeting 133
Wat
  Phra Keo 10, 24
  Phra That Doi Suthep 92, 94
water hazards
  Bangkapong Riverside 49
  Bangsai Country Club 34–5
  Blue Canyon 144–5, 146
  Chiangmai Green Valley 100
  Dynasty 28–9
  Eastern Star 74–5
  Green Valley 37
  Laem Chabang 66–7
  Lam Luk Ka 38–9
  Loch Palm 151
  Majestic Creek, The 130–31
  Natural Park Resort 60
  Navatanee 40–41
  Panya Park 42–3
  Pattaya Country Club 69
  Phoenix 71
  Phuket Country Club 147
  President Country Club 44–5
  Rose Garden, The 30–31
  Sawang Resort 135
  Thai
    Country Club 46–7
    Muang Beach 142–3
  Waterford Valley 104–5
Western
  Kanchanaburi 108–21
  region 122–37
wildlife 82, 140
Windmill Park Country Club 154
Woods, Tiger 9, 47